mediaworld

mediaworld
PROGRAMMING THE PUBLIC

JOHN M. PHELAN

A CONTINUUM BOOK
The Seabury Press   New York

1977
The Seabury Press
815 Second Avenue
New York, New York 10017

Printed in the United States of America

Library of Congress Cataloging in Publication Data

Phelan, John M   Mediaworld.
(A Continuum book)
1. Mass media—Social aspects. 2. Mass media—
Political aspects. 3. Popular culture. I. Title.
HM258.P475   301.16′1   76–56780   ISBN 0–8164–9317–0

Contents

PART THREE.
Beyond Mediaworld

Preface

Architects know that nothing is great or small, important or trivial, save for position. So it is with this book. It is a building made from available bricks, but the significance of the structure and the retrospective import of each brick are transformed by the overarching construction of the total design.

The concepts of celebrity, stardom, predictability, capital-intensity, political and social issues, mass production and mass distribution, for instance, are compartmentally clear and routinely accessible. But once it is seen that both public issues and celebrities are functionally identical instances of the star system —that the star system is a corollary to capital-intensive production for mass markets, and that, further, mass marketing has a relationship both to the idea of tradition and to the fact of population increase—then Daniel Boorstin's familiar observation that celebrities are people who are famous for being well-known takes on the air of an inevitable conclusion to a systematic necessity.

The idea of bureaucracy and the experience of entertainment are commonplace. But their strange marriage in the management halls of the mass media, colored lights flashing in little grey rooms, casts both the idea and the experience in novel and

mutually illuminating relief. So, too, the conflict between snob-
bery and populism, the revulsion of refinement for vulgarity,
are at least as old as Horace's *profanum vulgus.* Mass education
and mass media have placed this classic opposition in the tedious context of manufactured debate about the competing virtues and vices of elite and popular culture—a debate all too
often distorted by bizarre comparisons between, say, fox hunting and boxing, in sober search of socio-economic indicators for
aesthetic value. Shifting the controversy and the concern to a
new context, where popular culture is seen rather as a centrally
manufactured and globally distributed substitute for local community and as a subversion of tradition, elite or ethnic, awakens
new interest and new urgency in the debate. The frame of the
question is so altered that Bruno Bettelheim on fairy tales, for
example, becomes far more relevant and helpful than Gans on
"Taste Publics."

Everyone is unfortunately familiar with high food prices,
poisonous food additives, air and water pollution, clogged highways and clogged lungs. It was not until Barry Commoner's
The Closing Circle (and his more recent *The Poverty of Power*)
that the general public began to realize that these problems
were as intimately interconnected and systematic as the delicate
environment they continue to erode, constituting a sort of counter-ecology. It is the ambition and design of *Mediaworld* to
provide an analogously systematic context for understanding
the cultural and cognitive counter-ecology that increasingly
permeates our mental and moral environment.

mediaworld

part one
THE TECHNOLOGY OF OPINION

one
Melodoxy and Mediaworld

Historians and journalists are professionally interested in something that has been called the climate of opinion. The phrase refers to the prevailing psychic atmosphere, to commonly shared predispositions in evaluating certain aspects of life. Knowing the climate of opinion of a period is of immeasurable aid to the historian, for it provides him with a background that can give him perspective on the admittedly spotty and selected documents he must rely on. A journalist is equally concerned with the climate of opinion of his own time and place, or of the place he is assigned to cover. A proper feeling for the climate can guide his questioning to the currently defined heart of any matter.

Sociologists and psychologists, and even some philosophers, are directing increasing attention to what Peter Berger has described as cognitive style. It is the way people think about everyday things—their jobs, their wives, their children, their country. Cognitive style is in very large measure determined by the type of social organization within which people lead their lives and thus think their thoughts. Factory workers in Detroit have a cognitive style different from that of Tibetan yak herders.

Although climate of opinion and cognitive style are intimately related, they are distinct from one another. The former is more concerned with specific attitudes toward definite problems and questions that face groups. The latter is more related to the manner and method of dealing with enduring personal experiences.

A third and separate category of public discourse is also relevant here. A distinction has always been made between the careful expression of measured truths about the immediate evidence on any question, and careless swapping of gossip, superstition, hearsay, and unexamined folklore and prejudice about anything and everything. Plato placed the latter in the domain of *doxa*—(uninformed) opinion; Bacon spoke of the idols of the marketplace.

This book is about an elusive something that somehow is located among all three of these concepts. That something is the prevailing style of thought and method of argument, the collection of unexamined assumptions that determine questions before they are asked, the acceptable list of preferred topics at any one time, the intellectually fashionable and the broadly popular, trends and the legitimacy of accepting trends. It is the universe of discourse made possible—and perhaps required—by the mass communication systems of the production and distribution of ideas and sensibilities.

Elusive as it is, it is a unitary phenomenon deserving of a name, if only for the sake of simplicity. The name I have chosen is *melodoxy.* It has Greek roots, as in ortho-*doxy* and *melo* drama. In these times of controversy, we are familiar with "orthodox" and "heterodox" as the proper descriptions for opinions or activities that fit, or do not fit, the social context within which they are expressed. We are familiar with "melodrama" as a simplistic and stereotypical script of shallow characters in stark conflict according to a familiar pattern or plot. (*Melos,* Greek for song or melody, originally was placed before *drama* to describe seventeenth-century French popular dramas that featured songs throughout the performance.) Opinions that most easily fit mass media formats of presentation in style or content are melodox. Emotional responses that are most in keeping with the prevailing sensibilities found in mass-distributed TV drama, *Time* essays, syndicated columns, and, above all, advertising in print or on screen are also melodox. By its very nature, advertising is the epitome of the melodox.

Advertising is the major genre of art and writing today. It reaches the most people, commands the highest fees per word of any form of writing, receives by far the greatest technical artistry per minute in film and on sound, and has been a major influence on the style of speech and writing of virtually every class of person. The cinematic style that many novelists have adopted owes much to the montage effects of the television commercial. Clergymen and professors use advertising slogans to wryly make a point by lapsing below their expected level, even as ghetto residents carefully incorporate the same slogans in their conversation to show they are alert to the real. (Since there is such rapid turnover of slogans, any example in this book would soon be dated—itself a mark of the melodox—but a current ghetto synonym of "rapid" is "instamatic.")

Advertising copy must be brief, repetitious, attention-getting, and memorable. The jingle lends itself perfectly to all of these requirements, as all parents are painfully aware. Transparent subterfuge is permitted and expected, with emphasis exclusively on the positive. Thus diet drinks are promoted as "sugar-free," although loaded with chemicals of no food value, and candy is "energy-packed." The presence of caffeine is heralded as "that morning lift," and the absence of caffeine is "easy on the nerves."

Politicians, who must compete with product advertising, have not been slow to learn its methods. It is no wonder that Nixon could invoke the work ethic even as he froze wages and Johnson could promise both guns and butter without turning a hair. It is what we all expect. A masterpiece of melodoxy was achieved by a union leader in New York who stated that unless his demands were met "job action would increase to zero."

Melodoxy is thus the mental and emotional analogue of the slogan. It is fragmentary rather than whole. It is without precedent or conclusion. It is without patience or integrity. It is stereotypical and mechanistic. Essentially it is a method of avoiding analysis, or even notice, of the concrete particulars of any question or problem or experience by quickly categorizing it according to some well-known phrase which is seen as terminally lucid, although itself a fabrication of sophistry.

Melodoxy permits long conversations between lovers or strangers on virtually any topic without the least danger or evidence or thought, or even of moderate attention, arising. It enables editors and producers to come out with "in-depth" studies of virtually anything on a weekly, or even daily, schedule. A systematic necessity of media economics, melodoxy has become a characteristic of private as well as public discourse in our time. It has laid down the track which public opinion and popular culture both follow.

Although pre-melodoxical thinkers like Plato and Kant had to be content with lackluster concepts like the "idea of the good" and the "categorical imperative," current thought-smiths have given us the "effluent society," "arcology" (instead of "ecotecture"), and "generation gap"—the last, by melodoxical standards, a hoary perennial. Responsible office-holders have been able to share their plans and insights with all of us through the melodoxically rich concepts of "Russification" (Tsar Nicholas), "Vietnamization" (Nixon), "détente" (Kissinger), and "no free lunch" (Secretary Simon).

In the melodoxical world, mental and physical health can be achieved by effortless application of secret formulae and procedures revealed in books available at a local drugstore. Arcane methodologies, like having friends, getting enough sleep, eating a balanced diet, are detailed in graphic pamphlets on amicologizing, dormification, metromasticating. Finally, social and literary criticism have enlarged their audience and enriched their practitioners by judicious melodoxy. In the old days folks had to handle well wrought urns and sensate cultures; now they can deal with hot and cool messages, structures, zero degree, and metamyths.

It is even conceivable that a book on the nature and function of public opinion and popular culture within the mass communication system could be made more welcome in the marketplace by calling it an analysis of some bizarre neologism like, say, melodoxy.

Now that the point is made, the word will be retired from this volume.

This is not a book, therefore, about the media.

It is a book about the climate of opinion and cognitive style created by the media, within which we deal with "the world."

Now I look upon the world as made up of two parts. First, there is the world of problems and issues a society has to face. Second, there is the world of sense and sensibility in which an individual participates as observer and critic, as thinker and lover. For at least the last fifty years the former aspect of the world has increasingly been relegated to the arena we call "public opinion." The term "popular culture" has embraced that variety of artifacts, arts, and activities through which the vast majority of Americans develop most of their sensibilities and through which every American, without exception, acquires some of his sensibilities.

Both public opinion and popular culture are intimately, even essentially, interlocked within the media system, the modern mass production and mass distribution organizations that deal with information, ideas, and arts. Arranged in hierarchical corporate bureaucracies and utilizing very advanced technologies, the media system is at once the principal agent for and the prime example of the process of modernization.

There have been a number of separate books and articles written on all of these topics from disparate viewpoints. Books about public opinion tend to be political science studies of processes involving groups and interests in the confined arena of some form of -cracy, or ruling power: democracy, aristocracy, meritocracy, bureaucracy. Social psychology has a great interest in public opinion as the arena for personal attitude and opinion formation. Books about popular culture are either essays about the aesthetic standards embodied in so-called high culture and absent (or also present) in so-called low(brow) culture, or they are surveys of classes of people and the way they spend their time.

Books about the media are more varied in viewpoint, but generally they are either technical (legal, historical, economic, psychological, statistical) studies of media institutions, or bits of involved gossip about what goes on behind the scenes.

Walter Lippmann, the father of the sociopolitical use of the concept "stereotype" in the context of the print journalism of the 1920s, admirably succeeded in introducing fundamental concepts of ego-psychology (and common sense) into an understanding of the political journalism of his and of any time. Dwight Macdonald, the sixties' reviser of Van Wyck Brooks' three brows in the context of modern electronic and film media, most clearly articulated the lines of conflict in the popular-culture/elite-culture debate, with insightful generalities about the role of the middleman in the media system. Marshall McLuhan, a creature of the super-hype of the sixties, has made a less clear-cut contribution. I tend to agree with James Carey that as a performer (not as a thinker), McLuhan brilliantly popularized fellow Canadian Harold Adams Innis's thesis about the power of communication technology to shape society. At times arrogantly dismissed by the Academy for his admittedly theatrical presentations, McLuhan nonetheless set off timely sparks for a generation of serious students of the media and of American culture, with his outrageous puns and aphorisms.

This book seeks to present and examine the fundamental

unity of public opinion, popular culture, and the media system as the all-embracing determinants of our cognitive structure of the world.

The media condition our milieu in three ways. They provide the common background for a mobile people with no single distinctive cultural heritage. Second, they package ideas and events in a dramatic form that is brief, colorful, blandly controversial, and outside of any enduring context of value judgment. Finally, the media are part of a mass marketing system and thus view the public as an audience of potential customers for products.

These structural restrictions of the media system have a profound impact on our consciousness and on our culture. The impact resonates through public opinion and popular culture, which have been rendered less distinct from one another and less patient of analysis through the established paradigms of the social sciences and aesthetic criticism. News becomes entertainment rather than information, and entertainment carries a freight of information about public issues.

We are thus faced with the transformation of the traditional forum of public debate into a marketplace of competing commercial symbols; of seasons and festivals from yesteryear's traditions embalmed as occasions for advertising; of fantasy mixed with real events; of eternal human questions packaged as contemporary problems with solutions in terms of products or programs. It is revealing of this media transformation of our culture that lives are seen more in terms of roles, political events in terms of scenarios, and public figures as actors in a game.

So in this book I am going to talk about the media system, the cultural milieu created by the media, the self-fulfilling expectations of media middlemen about the audience (the public), and the very specific effects this has had on the transformation of public opinion and popular culture into one homogenized form-assumptive world: *Mediaworld.*

The purpose of the book is a modest one. There is no pretense of great revelations about the meaning of life in the seventies, or of the hitherto unimagined meaning of the media. Rather it is an attempt to offer a coherent single model of Mediaworld as a locus of explanation for what may seem, to others, a series of separate and unrelated phenomena. It is an organization of the obvious offered with the hope that it may give a more definite and articulate shape to what most of my readers may have felt on separate occasions and left in different compartments of experience.

Dealing with the obvious has its disadvantages. At times the sophisticated reader (and the unsophisticated reader perhaps more so) may wish that the text would simply get on with it and stop wasting time discovering the Tiber. It is like explaining an accident to an eyewitness. We have all been exposed to the media, therefore we presume that differences of perspective or emphasis about media content or methods are at most trivial. In the first analysis, they may be, but without correction they may lead to irrevocably divergent conclusions in the final analysis. I therefore ask the reader to be patient in the earlier parts of the text, where certain common ground is established rather than presumed.

Finally, in selecting instances from the electronic media, particularly television, to illustrate points, I have tried to select the "classic" rather than the immediately current. By "classic" I mean program formats that have been sufficiently popular for a truly mass audience over a number of years. Examples are useless unless they are familiar. What may be at the top of the ratings when the reader reads or the writer writes is too subject to change of time and place.

Finally, I have chosen John Stuart Mill's notion of the importance and function of free expression in a free society as a point of departure not because I believe his to have been either the first or last word on the matter, but merely because it seems to me, after two decades of close observation, that his formulations from *On Liberty* have served both high institutions and low individuals as a basic text of common ground in so much of the sound and sense, as well as of the fury, of current polemics.

two
A Free Marketplace of Issues

Over one hundred years ago John Stuart Mill passionately insisted that freedom of expression and full and frank debate of every imaginable issue was at the heart of human freedom itself. The freedom he had in mind was individualistic. Everyone should be free "to pursue his own good in his own way." For Mill, this was the raison d'être of society, to promote and protect the individual. Concomitantly, healthy individuals, freely expressing their inmost ideas, were the mainstay of society, urging progressive and daring policies in an atmosphere of fearless debate.

These basic ideas, not original to Mill but best formulated by him, are still with us today. They form the fundamental creed of journalists, who profess it often. They frame the philosophy behind the Fairness Doctrine of the Federal Communications Commission and the tacit regionalism of the Public Broadcasting Corporation. Although Mill wrote long after the debates about and the enactment of the First Amendment, most of the First Amendment decisions of this century, from Holmes' celebrated "clear and present danger" test to the Pentagon Papers case, repeat in some form his notions of the sacredness of free expression. Even Captain Kirk of the starship *Enterprise* is wont to chide alien civilizations for their failure to adhere to the

Millsian canon, which it is part of his mission to bring to the whole galaxy.

The addition of the fictional Captain Kirk as an exponent of political philosophy and the fact that he is better known than Oliver Wendell Holmes to many journalists and television news producers are signs of something new that Mill could not have foreseen, as well as evidence of the pervasiveness of his ideas as the current form of the orthodox creed.

For although the ideals and stated functions of public debate may have been formulated in the nineteenth century, following a long tradition begun in Athens, the forum and setting for public debate have changed radically. So great is the transformation of the forum that public debate and the freedom it requires have themselves undergone profound transformation. Although the transformation is only too carefully taken into account in practice, it is frequently ignored in discussions of principle and philosophy, thus creating a chasm greater than usual between what is professed and what is practised. This same blind spot also renders many discussions of ethics in public matters irrelevantly ritualistic.

Although virtually every feature of our current forum of public opinion is familiar, it will be helpful for the later argument to organize these features into a coherent model.

THE PASSING OF THE TRADITIONAL FORUM

A convenient way to describe any transformation is to postulate a clear and simple paradigm of the prior state and an equally clear and simple paradigm of the subsequent state and contrast the two. Once this is done, details can be added to the skeletal sketch. Let me call the earlier forum of public opinion traditional; and the subsequent and current forum, transitional.

The traditional forum as an ideal type would in the impossible extreme have no room for private opinion at all. Everything not forbidden would be compulsory. Every public policy, every pattern of private life would be culturally determined, a simple given, unquestioned as the phases of the moon. Nothing can be utterly static, however, and new events and problems will arise for which there is no cultural rule, no exact precedent. In the face of these problems, honest men, of the same background and education, can differ. They will debate, according to rules and protocols clearly understood by all, what course of action should be taken. That which seems most sensible to the majority will be the course adopted.

In this traditional forum the people are members of a community of shared values. They are organized hierarchically into groups of face-to-face individuals. Each group is led by someone whose views in general, or at least on any given type of issue, are respected because he is more informed, more involved, better educated, endowed perhaps with some elusive character that makes him persuasive: dignity, position, charm, charism.

In the usual analysis the leaders are scattered throughout the mass of America, transforming an undifferentiated and homogeneous loaf into disparate slices with their own distinctive texture and flavor. Thus the nation can engage in great debates: about war and peace, about poverty, about slavery, about race, about pollution, about energy, even about personal honesty and sexual morality. It forms a collective of manageable cells, each debating in an intimate traditional forum matters of local, national, international import.

The cartoon of this concept—and in our image-dominated time the cartoon controls the concept all too often—is embedded in the imagination of moviegoers by Capra and his school of sentimentality about the Little People of Democracy. Spinning newspaper headlines sprout from the screen; fedora-clad heads incline intently to Emerson radio speakers; motorists at gas stations, women at garden clubs, office workers in elevators, all voice in breathtaking rapidity and startling simplicity a common will for some new person, or policy, or product. Such a process of public opinion as the traditional forum encompasses, whether practised by an elite as envisaged by Mill (who may well have relegated Capra's crowds to the "backward states" not ready for self-rule) or by a New England town meeting, assumes a commonality of values, of goals, of political vision. However, any visitor to a public hearing about, say, utility rates—to pick a relatively clear-cut conflict—would witness a procedure poles apart from the traditional forum. He would see paid performers, scripted argument, histrionic exhibitionism, virtuoso gestures of deception: a variety of immovable rocks encountered by rationally irresistible forces. It is a scene not for Mill, but for Kafka or Camus.

Thus the classic paradigm of public opinion as an enclosed debate, following cultural rules of behavior and discourse, about a definite question of clearly perceived policy, involving organized groups with historical roots, leading to a practical compromise through political mechanisms such as representative bodies and mandated executives—this traditional forum, if it ever could have existed—has surely vanished.

The abstract paradigm of the transitional forum for public opinion is quite different. Here the culture has run out of legitimating steam for the smooth operation of all the arrangements for doing things that are commonly accepted in the traditional forum. Everything is debatable, nothing is taken for granted. This ideal type could not of course exist in pure form any more than could the traditional type. Where the latter would stagnate into decaying immobility, the former would be frozen in panic-stricken aboulia. Nothing could happen.

Some experimental colleges of the sixties tried to bring this transitional forum, in its extreme type, into incarnate life. They failed. There were meetings about what should be studied. Then there had to be further meetings about the necessity of agreeing whether or not all had to study one thing together. Soon there were discussions about discussions until the entire group shattered into isolated and catatonic chips.

Short of this catastrophic extreme, the transitional forum seems to mark many of the current features of contemporary opinion—its climate, if not its weather.

It used to be a cliché characterization of a politician who sought to please all and offend none to say that he was against sin and for motherhood. Now he would no longer be quite so safe, since both sin and motherhood, as media anchorpersons are wont to say, are controversial issues.

Cultural rules, the very substance and boundaries of the traditional forum, are matters for debate in the transitional forum. Debate, as a method of arriving at decisions, is debatable. Whether we wish to assign the occasion of the demise of the traditional forum to Khruschev's shoe-banging at the United Nations, or to Mark Rudd's telling the president of Columbia University, panoplied with overwhelming traditional authority, to attempt the anatomically absurd on his own body, it is clear that public opinion now covers a far wider area of concern than it ever did before. Its processes are no longer polite, nor are they under some commonly accepted cultural arbitration.

Judges in court now must rule on whether little girls can play baseball with little boys or whether male dancers must wear token brassieres to equalize treatment of the sexes. This loss of cultural confidence heralds more than the collapse of procedures for deciding issues. It marks the death of the very concept of issue as a feature of public consciousness. Ironically, just when we have reached a pass when no more genuine issues face genuine publics with alternate choices based on informed opinions, we are told that we live in an issue-oriented society embroiled in controversy.

"Issue," one of the most frequently invoked words of the century in the media, is a cornerstone of the conventional wisdom in that the frequency of its invocation is in direct proportion to the rarity of its being examined. In a way, the idea of issue parallels the idea of stereotype, in Lippmann's original sense.

Stereotypes are useful necessities to help people deal with the complexity of the world by selecting and simplifying the overwhelming amount and variety of material that assaults them directly and through the media. Selection and simplification are dangerous mental habits only if they are not acknowledged for what they are: regrettably necessary conveniences that enable people to encounter life, albeit provisional in the face of efforts to understand totally any aspect we wish to experience fully.

Issues serve a similar function. Issues are the simplified and selected questions that match the simplified and selective statements of stereotypes. Issues are indispensable to decision-making. "Fish or cut bait." That there are actually a multitude of options between the reality of angling and the reality of preparing worms is irrelevant to the decision-maker. Public debate selects views in order to reach decisions; the multiplicity of public policy alternatives is simplified and sharpened by debate to clear-cut dichotomies: war or peace, save or spend, hire or fire.

According to the traditional wisdom, a politician was wise to identify himself with the winning side of an issue that attracted the widest possible public among the electorate: the full-employment candidate, the peace-in-our-time candidate. Present day office-seekers must yearn for those imagined good old days of taking a stand to win over the majority who already were persuaded of the merits of the case, and thus of the merits of the man who espoused it.

It is true that some genuine issues still survive on the very local level where discussions can take place among face-to-face publics about immediate and tangible problems. Increasing interdependence, however, as spectacularly brought to prominence in the financial ruin of New York City and its effects on scores of smaller municipalities, has reduced most of these issues to the relatively trivial, such as the location of traffic lights and the budgets of small libraries. Little else gets debated in the sense Mill envisioned.

People no longer form publics, although they may belong to militant organizations with demands for themselves, quite divorced from any sense of the common weal. They may also feel vaguely part of some movement, like consumerism. Issues supposedly focus communities into purposeful publics. What now pass for issues rarely serve this function.

As the traditional model of public opinion yielded to the transitional phase, candidates for all but the most parochial offices felt pressured to adopt stands not on issues of policy but on deeply divisive cultural clashes of fundamental principle and value: the anti-sexist candidate, the liberal-radical candidate, the free-enterprise candidate, the countercultural candidate. Issues were beginning to melt and fade into vague wraiths of attitudes toward the meaning of life in general: the candidate of love, the candidate of hope and honesty. Specific questions about abortion, or arms appropriations, or industrial regulation were beginning to change their function. As issues—the formulation of realistic policy alternatives that embody coherent political philosophies, or even compelling partisan loyalties—they failed. These questions, in reality, were too complex, too subject to vast bureaucratic mechanisms that diluted and transformed the intended effects of executive decisions; they were too involved with labyrinthinely interlocked economic sectors, producing paradoxical results, to truly test the stand or stance of a politician, even if he were candid. The specific questions were no longer the issues they had been in the simpler and tidier traditional forum. In the new public opinion, the questions were rather promptings for the public unveiling of personality traits: compassion, sincerity, vigor, wit, intelligence.

In the transitional forum, it is as if the electorate were saying: we don't know what he will do; we don't know what he or anyone can do; but we think he is a good man, we trust him;

he wishes us no harm. Instead of leaders forming publics by taking stands on genuine issues, politicians perform for audiences who will mark them on their charm and, above all, on their sincerity—a paradoxical criterion for what can only be called an "act." Both major candidates in the 1976 presidential campaign had full-time staff members appointed as officers of "issue development." Such aides have become most helpful as talking about "issues" has replaced deciding on policies.

This is a profound change in public consciousness and in the very meaning and purpose of the so-called forum of public opinion. Like any such radical transformation, it came about gradually, but dawned on us suddenly. Although the causes are manifold, they are of two principal types.

The first type is in the nature of modernization: complex and bureaucratic social organization combined with high technology. Nothing in modern society is simple and clear-cut; every policy has unforeseen results. Baffling complexity is an obvious contributor to the death of genuine issues as stimulants to effective political action. But modernization, of course, is a vast backdrop to all the events and befuddlements of the century. The second type of cause is far more direct and immediate: it is in the nature of modern communication.

STELLAR CONCEPTS

To match the vast complex technical order of modern society, there is a vast complex technical communication system. The part of the system that presents so-called issues to the so-called public is totally dominated by the methods and mentality of marketing. The wire services, the newsmagazines, the networks and their lesser local satellites are termed the mass media for good reason: they mass-produce for mass audiences and harvest mass money. Produced and distributed by and through mass media, the issues of the transitional forum are creatures of mass marketing necessities.

The basic task of mass marketing is to please vast numbers of customers with a standardized, predictable, and enduring product. The product must be standardized because of the vast quantities that must be made, harvested or cooked. It must be predictable so that the mass of consumers will get exactly what they expect again and again, forming a habit, preferably for life, of brand loyalty. As more and more products are mass-marketed to larger and larger markets, the world becomes populated with ever greater armies of identical units. Coca-Cola was the early symbol of this process of repetitive ubiquity, as McDonald's hamburgers are today. Even natural goods, however, are subject to the same procedures. The apple, once present all over America in literally hundreds of sizes and textures and tastes, has been simplified to a few types for the sake of standardization, predictability, and longer life between picking and eating, for vast quantities travel thousands of miles to market.

If mass production requires standardization and predictability, it must be matched by standard and especially predictable consumption. Demand must be managed by creating needs through advertising. These obvious generalities are clear when it comes to soap or automobiles. They are equally operative in show business, particularly in the logic of the star system, originated in the theater and spread to film, television, and publishing. Despite the best efforts of the large companies and banks that either own or invest in films, they cannot be made standard and predictable products with a managed demand that guarantees sales. Each film is different. But stars endure. Money spent promoting the image and glamor and desirability of a star can bring returns over many years and be transferred to the vehicle they appear in. Stars are standard and predictable ingredients. That is why so many cowboys and detectives and lovers of stage and screen keep right on working long past decent retirement. That is why the sons and daughters of stars are preferred to utterly new units requiring expensive promotion.

Stardom, from the point of view of marketing, is a method

of introducing standardization, predictability, endurance, and demand management into the intangible and evanescent realm of art and entertainment. The news and information business, with capital costs and marketing needs paralleling those of the entertainment business, also deals in the impalpable and especially in the unpredictable—the events of the day. It is clear that it must use some form of the star system, and the promotion of news "personalities" is an increasing characteristic of TV news and print columns. The most successful adaptation of the star system, however, is the conversion of "issues" from questions of public moment to methods of packaging information with some measure of sales predictability.

Coca-Cola, McDonald's hamburgers, Paul Newman, Walter Cronkite, Sex in Washington, Pollution—this disparate list of things, persons and issues serves the common function of guaranteeing future sales to the vehicles they are in, or to the units that distribute them.

Common issues enable media owners and managers to spread out the cost of promotion for their units and vehicles. The interest generated by one medium in any given issue serves as a stimulus for purchase of a different medium dealing with the same issue. This is no secret to buyers of paperback versions of movies they have just seen. Current issues enable newsmagazine editors and broadcast assignment editors to plan future editions and programs with some idea of their sales potential.

As with stars, issues are kept in circulation as long as possible, for continued maximum return on promotional investment and maximum mileage out of the efforts of complementary and competing media. Issues are magnified and recycled relentlessly. It is this characteristic that has perhaps prompted Michael Arlen to say that we have never been exposed to more news, and yet we have never felt so ignorant. We are exposed to a great quantity of verbiage and images, but it is frequently the reworking of a stock issue, spawning repetition without development and exposure without absorption.

Andy Warhol's celebrated conceit, that in the future every-one will be world-famous, but only for fifteen minutes, was probably suggested by the common characteristic of stars and issues. His comment is misleading, however, if taken to mean that mass production, and thus mass media, are eager for quick changes of product. Mass marketing of goods and people and ideas requires quick turnover of sales, but preferably of the same product endlessly repeated. With unconscious candor, the media have spoken of the "issues of the seventies," thus hoping for a ten-year shelf life that has thus far eluded the chemists of agribusiness and the designers of Detroit.

John Stuart Mill saw public debate in terms of the market-place. In the free competition of truth and error, truth would win out. It was the marketplace of Adam Smith, and it was a metaphor. Today public debate can again be seen in terms of the marketplace, but the marketplace is now the modern one of managed demand, of need created by advertising. It is the marketplace of John Kenneth Galbraith this time, and it is not just a metaphor. Issues are not *like* products, with the truth, like the better mousetrap, winning the adherence of honest men of logical mien by its intrinsic virtue. Issues *are* products. They are for sale. They are advertised. A need is created to know *about* them. They are consumed like so many Delicious applies; they do not lead to anything beyond themselves.

Early in the seventies a sample of midwestern Americans was asked to rank in order the most important issues facing the nation. The answers were then compared with an analysis of the coverage given to issues on the part of major media. There was almost a perfect correspondence between the rank order derived from polling the people and the rank order of media coverage. This was heralded as a mark of how well the public was served by the media, until a sceptical researcher ap-proached a similar sample of Americans and asked them what worried them the most. The rank order of these concerns was at considerable variance from that of media coverage. For these

Americans, important issues were what the media were considering important. Matters that required some practical resolution, some public action, were of a different sort.

In preparation for coverage of the 1976 national elections, CBS News commissioned a poll to determine what issues (their term) were paramount in the voters' minds and therefore would require attention from the candidates. The issues most frequently cited were the "energy crisis," "unemployment," "inflation," and "crime control."

These of course are not issues. They are topics; they are problem areas; they are sources of concern. Issues are sharp specific questions leading to some kind of practical decision that can be implemented in policy and in practice. But for CBS News, for the candidates, and for the media audience these were the issues in the very important sense that these would be the headings for news coverage, the source of speech material, the topics for conversation. In effect an issue has become the very thing about which we can *do* nothing, but about which we can speak.

Pointing out that the meaning of issue and its true function are now in terms of marketing rather than of the dynamics of public opinion in a democratic society does not imply that the topics so marketed do not indeed envelop the possibility of true discussion, that they might not contain genuine issues, leading to choices among genuine policy alternatives. Yet, the complexities of government, the problems it must deal with, *and* the nature of the media have made this very unlikely. Issues now are more like the assigned topics of high school debate, with attention on the playing of the game, not the outcome—for there is no outcome. As a 1976 campaign worker put it: an issue is anything your opponent is afraid to talk about.

The concept of issue was the pivotal notion of the traditional stage of public opinion as Mill saw it. The American Civil Liberties Union, the Office of Communication of the United Church of Christ, the Federal Communications Commission,

the Supreme Court of the United States—these varied and influential institutions all assume that public opinion is still in
that stage and they work mightily to establish conditions where
freedom of expression will flourish, believing that thus public
opinion will thresh out the truth and inform public policy. Our
cultural condition, however, militates against freedom of expression for opinions as a precondition to democratic debate.
There are no more opinions in the classic sense. There is advo-
cacy, there is controversy, there is conflict, there is special
pleading. The halls of government and the heads of citizens
reverberate with a shattering overload of loud talk and es-
calated rhetoric of partisan denunciation. But there is no joining of issues. There is a moment in court for a parade of uncom-
promising cases, presented as fact rather than opinion.

The shift from the traditional stage of Mill, where differences
of *opinion* (views based on values drawn from philosophies)
would be encouraged, to the current media-dominated transitional stage where contrasting viewpoints and positions (specific goals sought for reasons of self-interest, prejudice, or even
taste) are temporally (broadcasting) or spatially (print) jux-
taposed, has brought about a shift in the understanding of
freedom of expression. Mill felt that this freedom was essential,
for it gave an outlet and a social goal to thought, the distinctive
mark of humanity. It was the removal of outside restraint to let
a hundred flowers bloom. Now the emphasis is on access to the
media and access to the *facts*. The contemporary conviction is
that positions are entitled to support (rather than that opinions
deserve a hearing).

The result is that those who live in large cities are bombarded
by a multimedia barrage of Babel under the aegis of promoting
controversy, giving the superficial impression of the lively and
vigorous diversity of views about public issues so desired by
liberals who are Mill's spiritual heirs. But there is little debate;
there is not even much contact. Instead there is a dramatic
conflict of *personalities* (not persons) who ride ideas the way

Tom Mix rode horses. The ultimate cartoon of this development is the staged contrast of Shana Alexander and Jackson Kilpatrick in opposing liberal/conservative corners. Their segments (broadcast at the end of CBS's excellent feature story series, "60 Minutes") are videotaped separately. They rarely are in the same studio, but they face to opposite sides, giving the viewer the illusion of conversation. So we don't even have conversation, let alone genuine controversy—we have willing players in a game of issue-mongering.

Daniel Boorstin pointed out long ago that reporters and politicians frequently concocted controversies to promote sales, ratings, and votes in one symbiotic, and very fell, swoop. Few could have foreseen the media reflex that this has become. Not only is the public ignorant, though exposed to so much (repetitious and undeveloped) "news," it is also unstimulated to thought or to any democratic action by genuine debate. Although the airwaves crackle with the sound of arguing, there is rarely an argument. Moderators on talk shows squirm and fidget when the dread possibility of serious (intellectual) intercourse looms. In the action-news format, two hapless professors can often be surrounded, as it were, by one nervous interlocutor who in effect demands that they "say something controversial," the way the vaudeville stage father would ask his educated son to "say something French."

Overwhelmed by such a welter of noise, more and more groups want to add their own note to the silly symphony. By no means is this meant to patronize many groups whose causes are just and who are really and truly cut off from any hearing because of corporate domination of the airwaves (where competition is often regulated out of existence and the entry price demands a lot of capital). The point is that their case becomes just another bicentennial minute so that their argument cannot be heard and thus cannot be judged.

Argument and true debate exist only in a universe of discourse where there are standards of judgment. Unless these

standards are commonly accepted by a community with historical roots, they are merely academic.

Such a community of common standards was a feature of the
traditional stage of public opinion. It no longer applies to the
current transitional stage. Thus there is a closed loop. Media
economics foster issue-mongering; the media are part of a high-
technology society where solutions and policies are too complex
for reduction to genuine *public* issues; the prevalence of media-
packaged issues makes it hard for the public to conceive of a
debate that is not a conflict of personalities. The absence of
standards forces one's judgment back in the first instance on
personal qualities of beauty, trustworthiness, sincerity, charm,
wit, intelligence. The only other recourse for judgment is simple
factual truth, devoid of philosophy or party.

THE POINT OF FACTS

So, in addition to the desire to give different people access to
the media so that their personal qualities can be assessed, there
is increasing emphasis on the public's right to know. To know
what really happened. To know the true statistics of unemployment, or of body counts in war, or of Pentagon cost overruns.
To know whether a phone was tapped, or whether a man was
executed. Paradoxically, the government seems less reluctant to
permit any kind of opinion as an exercise in free speech, even
though it may be obscene, scandalous, blasphemous, libelous to
the government and its officials, than it is to tolerate the reporting of certain facts. The Pentagon Papers, if published as one
more voluminous disgorgement of the Government Printing
Office, would probably have attracted little notice. Smuggled
out by a disaffected public official (who was given the star
treatment for about three years) as a secret, the Pentagon Papers attracted wide attention as a *fact.* The syndrome has been
repeated (predictably) by the Nixon Tapes, the FBI Media
(Pennsylvania) Files, the Pike Committee Report on the CIA

and FBI, and numerous other leaks about facts of decisions made by Kissinger, Nixon, Rockefeller, Boards of Education, high corporate management. Grand jury testimony, a sacred secret, is under great pressure for publication, because of the overwhelming feeling that the public has a right to know.

As the forum of public opinion has become transitional, as the issue has become topic rather than task, the public has shifted to the role of passive knower. No longer is the public seen as a collection of interest groups who seek knowledge to form issues for decision-making. The public is offended simply because it is not informed of what decisions are already made or are about to be made. That these decisions must and will be made by officials for their own reasons is taken for granted. Their discourtesy, not their power, is resented.

The point is reinforced by the consequences of the revelations. The release of the Pentagon Papers did not spark renewed debate on the policy of waging war in the Far East. It sparked discussion about revealing government reports. Not many people outside of the reluctant Congress, who covered their eyes like Victorian gentlemen passing a bathhouse, actually read the Nixon transcripts, as opposed to the packaged presentations of the media. After a spate of devastatingly outrageous revelations about illegal and immoral leadership actions, from the "oil crisis" to the creative bookkeeping of the New York City Financial Administration, business is pretty much going on as usual for all of the *public* outrage ritually presented through the media.

The Freedom of Information Act, revised in 1975, does make it marginally less difficult to get at files and records of government that are not national security matters. Yet, if the past is any guide, then even more government data will be unearthed and used by big business, which is the overwhelmingly predominant, and highly sophisticated, employer of the Act's provisions favoring revelations of former secrets.

The growth and increasing strength of three bureaucracies

have gradually stifled and all but extinguished the vitality of public opinion. The government bureaucracy and the corporate bureaucracies have both withheld and dispensed information not to inform but to control. The media bureaucracies have revealed the secrets of the other bureaucracies too often within the antique context of the *scoop,* with emphasis on speed and sensationalism, because both characteristics are required for the strength and growth of the media business. Issue-mongering, an economic necessity for the media bureaucracies and a political expediency for government and corporations, has become an art of manipulation. Although different, even rival, all three are essentially devoted to controlling publics by turning them into nothing but paying (or voting) customers in a passive audience. All three bureaucracies assign a heavy portion of their budgets to processing and shaping information, and in many instances the government and major business corporations have more media specialists than the media themselves. So many highly skilled writers and film makers are so deviously busy telling their employers' "side of the story" that the public hears all side and no story.

The sincere concern previously noted for freedom of expression in America is often muddled, therefore, because it assumes the universe of the traditional forum for public opinion, when in fact we are in the transitional stage. The concern itself has been commercially exploited in a way that hastens the demise of what Mill treasured in a free society: the cultivation of reflection and learning and a sense of common weal and public decency. In this country at times it seems that the great media machine, the high technology of image-making and distribution, the precious preservation of First Amendment rights, are all in existence only to make sure that pornographers can turn a dollar.

As Isaiah Berlin has remarked, Mill lived in a claustrophobic period, the height of the long bourgeois Sunday afternoon, stiff-collared and bustled. In Victoria's time there was a crying need for the assertion of the beauty and vitality of individual differences to prevent a society from choking on its own righteousness. Our time, our stage, is agoraphobic. There is now a plethora of individuals "pursuing their own good in their own way," but they are doing so on an empty field. They are atoms, alone in an absolute state, without a locus for loyalty.

Debates need debating societies, some form of Nisbet's "social bond." Without a place, no point can be made. We are left with curiosity about facts and interest in personalities as performers in a game.

Meanwhile, earnest players with a very clever "game plan," very concerned with how their news theatre would play in Peoria, almost took over the country as armies of commentators were reveling in the promotion of "healthy diversity."

Socrates would not have been asked to depart or take hemlock in our transitional forum. He would have been taken out to lunch and offered a package deal for some of his dynamite ideas.

three
Protean Publics and Propaganda

Some years ago Bernard Berelson discussed what he was pleased to call the democratic personality and its relationship to the theory of public opinion. The theory he dealt with was much akin to what I have called the traditional forum. Berelson spoke of the democratic personality in terms of fairness, moral idealism, belief in reason, and faith in the wisdom of the majority. In short, he deduced virtues for his construct from the systematic necessities of the traditional forum.

In like manner, one can derive certain individual characteristics that make it more harmonious and suitable for people to live and think within the current transitional forum of public opinion. The atmosphere of packaged issues, passive publics, orchestrated special pleading, and simple loss of cultural confidence may lead to certain dominant types of individuals who help make what they are made by.

Romans may well have believed that it was sweet and fitting to die for their fatherland. Crusaders may have felt that God Himself was urging them to embark for Jerusalem. Some Americans may still feel that their lives may well be spent to make the world safe for democracy. But not very many.

Some would place the blame (or award the merit) for this loss of transcendence of the self to recent events unmercifully and relentlessly chronicled: Vietnam, which won no hearts nor minds, but squandered blood and treasure; and Watergate, which forced public focus on the heartless nihilism behind the political rhetoric of our time. Others would consider these events mere catalysts for a long and inevitable historical development. The democratization of education, the growth of industrialism, the introduction of objectifying techniques in the management of human affairs, the internationalism of business, and the interculturalism of communication—all of these marks of the First World remove individuals from their isolated nests and deprive them of the illusion that their own experience is either normative or inevitable.

This alienation creates a certain nostalgia for times and places of parochial certainties. Such romantic longings provide one explanation for the otherwise baffling sympathy and admiration for the draconian administration of China. Heads, like eggs, may have had to be broken, but the trains run on time, there are no slums, and the warlords are gone. The concern for the hive as a whole, the corporate dedication of old people and children, the evidences of cooperation and the absence of competition in its more obvious forms—these characteristics charm Western eyes, although they are at the same time seen to be hopelessly naïve for our own system and time, given our history and our institutions.

From the current perspective of disillusionment, it seems that men no longer live or die for ideas, if indeed they ever did. Rather, they live and they die (or, less grandly, they work and they pay) for other men who have been clever enough to employ ideas to motivate their labor and sacrifice. Along with lack of trust in other men, therefore, there is a loss of faith in ideas as instruments of progress and idealism. Ideas are mere building blocks for ideologies; ideals are means to motivate the many to serve the few.

Larger entities—tribes, churches, companies, countries—demand sacrifice so that they might prosper and endure. Yet the perpetuation of that very prosperity seems to be purchased only at the price of the poverty or extinction of some rival tribe, church, company, or country. The self-effacing altruism demanded of individuals is spectacularly absent in the larger entity which expands and triumphs. Growth of knowledge and the removal of cultural ghettos brought about by modern transportation and communication technologies have made it hard for an ever increasing number of people to accept the unique virtue of their own collectivity, worthy of unqualified allegiance.

Robert Jay Lifton, the psychiatrist who has made a profound study of the means used by China to maintain the largest example of sober solidarity known to man, looks upon such total loyalty as a form of pathology, which he has called the psychology of totalism. On philosophical and historical grounds, Isaiah Berlin is of the same opinion. To think that there is one best way of life for which sacrifices are in order is a constant in human affairs and a constant tragedy. There is no harmony of human ends, Berlin believes, but rather a staggering multiplicity of possibilities. It is therefore the mark of a truly civilized man to be willing to die for an ideal that he knows is provisional and thus in some measure illusory.

Mass education and mass media have diffused this fear of loyalty and dread of being taken for a fool on populations without the background or security or status that provide the conditions for the very rare version of "truly civilized man" Berlin presents. Working-class veterans of Vietnam, the sacrificial "grunts" in a war plotted and planned in Berkeley and Cambridge and the Pentagon, maimed and blinded, paralyzed and impotent, are not about to dance to the next piper's tune of glory. Thrifty middle-class elders, impoverished by inflation and fraudulent pension plans, moved on and out of active participation, are all the more bitter because their awakening came too late. It is one thing for an associate professor to bite his pipe stem in anguish over his alienation; it is quite another for an assembly-line worker in Detroit, or Stockholm, to see no purpose in his life, when he already knew there was no point to his job. As a consolation for living, both the professor and the worker demand all the money they can get. Money has become the great motivator, because all money now holds the promise and relief of "mad" money. It enables the owner to pursue loneliness, in Slater's phrase, through independence by means of possessions: the private house, the private car, the personal phone, the individual TV set, the villa, the yacht. It gives freedom to escape from one's condition and climate, even from one's mate and offspring (or parents). Cash makes lack of loyalty a virtue.

If loss of stable community and historical roots have made of mobility a necessity; if loss of cultural confidence has made of loyalty a folly, then the last escape is from the very sense of self. As a result, people do not see themselves so much leading lives as assuming roles. The descriptive rhetoric of personal behavior assumes loss of enduring identity and a context of play-acting to meet novel and evanescent situations, from the transactional school of therapy to the Goffman typologies of encounter. Lifton, in keeping with the adaptive biases of traditional psychiatry, has called for a conscious development of a psychology of acceptance of perpetual flux. This "protean man" will be immune to "future shock" and will know how to play a variety of successive roles with both style and satisfaction.

All of the basic characteristics of the transitional forum—the news theatre of pseudo-events, the mass production of packaged issues, the demand management of information, the public as audience—are matched by the transient personalities of protean people.

Within this kind of forum and among these kinds of individuals, forms of public communication take on the functions and features of propaganda. And, ultimately, the public dominates the private as the model of behavior and communication.

PROPAGANDA AND PRODUCTS

Jacques Ellul has distinguished two types of propaganda: agitative and integrative. The first type tries to get people to change, to stir them up perhaps to the point of revolution. The second type is designed to keep people as and where they are, to accept their life, even to be grateful for it: to conform cheerfully. In both types the cardinal mark of propaganda is present —the control of behavior through the control of belief. The evil of propaganda is not that it is false. It is its indifference to the very question of truth. Human expression is seen merely as a means, as an instrument, to get people to do what is desired. It is an indifference to truth that is also a denial, perhaps even a hatred, of human freedom. For the purposes of his propaganda, the propagandist must assume that his audience, his "target," as market research tellingly describes it, is something less than human: a mere collection of predictable responses, given the proper stimuli.

Propaganda is not human persuasion. It does not seek to win over an equal by argument, or even by appeal to the emotions, if emotions are understood as human emotions that are part of rational human organic experience. Propaganda assumes its target to be mechanistic. It does not win minds and hearts; it manipulates drives and needs.

The manager of a mass medium cannot think of his audience as individuals with individual tastes, preferences, quirks, ideals, and convictions. He must think of them as a market that must be managed to act predictably. Perhaps each individual may be free in some philosophic sense for which the manager has no time. Nevertheless, the mass, the market as a whole, can and must be studied scientifically in laboratory and in the field. Individuals, in this paradigm, cannot be of any more significance than separate coffee beans which must meet certain standards in order to be roasted and packaged under a brand name that is respected for its predictable flavor.

In the world of the total market, the need for predictability of sales requires that the buyer, as well as the product, be standardized and controlled. It is clear that wine tasters are measuring and certifying wine. But when a mass product, such as a new processed food, is test-marketed, the buyers have been as carefully chosen and tested as the product. In many cases, they are more tested than the product. The result is a transaction—a sale—in which two objects of mass management, people and products, interface in a neatly controlled exchange.

The mass media are the supreme means of arranging this interface. New pilots for television series are frequently tested before carefully selected audiences. The audience is wired for its reaction to the program. There is a "free" response and there is an automatic response. Heartbeat, respiration rate, galvanic skin response are tracked for each person automatically during the running of the pilot. Members of the audience are also given a lever, or button, which they can press along a gradient of degrees to indicate their pleasure or displeasure as the program proceeds. The entire input of this many-headed wired thing is averaged out to one giant reaction to the program and placed on graph paper matching each sprocketed moment of the pilot film. In Texas, a similar service measures and computes wired teen-agers' reactions to rock music before albums are released.

The service enables producers to remove material that fails to get the proper reaction and to expand and emphasize material that promotes the reaction they seek. The service also matches certain kinds of material to certain types of audiences. For while producers may be selling programs to networks or tapes to record publishers, the networks are selling audiences to advertisers and the major music publishers require definite demographics for their all-important radio airplay, also related to advertising. The real buyers, the audience buyers, want to know about their product.

Parallel research and demographic services are used by the top fifty magazines, from newsmagazines and business reports to "issue-oriented" slicks and girlie-gadget magazines, in their efforts to attract the heavy advertisers. Computers provide the service's customers with ludicrous particularities. How many dentists who drink scotch east of the Ohio River and who own two cars and a power mower buy a given magazine is the type of read-out that can be obtained. If a rival magazine is equal in all other respects, but does not have those dentists, then it may lose an advertiser.

Thus, wholesale traders in images and audiences—creative directors, time-buyers, promotion managers, et al.—combine to generate a sort of Platonic Form of the transitional forum. Color-coded fact books, bogus charts with magnificent graphics, industrial films, musical comedies and live entertainment of Las Vegas standards are part of the arsenal of persuasion used by master manipulators, working on one another in an atmosphere of tacit rules and devised glitter that recalls the court of Louis XIV.

The purpose of the whole game is to provide marketing managers with defensible business reasons for their choice of programs, music, magazines. It provides a bottom line for a media decision, as the jargon has it. Now the bottom line is a line of numbers. Ultimately, therefore, the various marketing services provide managers with numbers. As a result, it is possible, it is even desirable, to program 168 hours of television a week without ever bothering to see any of the film or tape, or without ever reading a script. It is simply a matter of picking big numbers over small numbers, for share of audience, advertising rates, and small numbers over big numbers for cost of production, rentals, royalty fees. Other numbers—detailing available capital and rival programming statistics—are also necessary. The arrangements of the numbers may be intricate —but numbers are being arranged, ideas are not being discussed.

The lamentably familiar mini-drama within one-minute or

30-second commercials, serves as an allegory for the entire system of which it is a bright and colored cog. The cast is basically three people: the buyer or user, who represents the viewer at home for whom the commercial is made and targeted, the best friend or close associate of the viewer/buyer, the authoritative salesperson (sometimes disembodied as a god-like voice-over).

Buyer has a problem with a thing (car, washing machine, sink drain) that is reaching desperate proportions. Best Friend shows up with thing totally under control. Best Friend reveals that product for sale is solution to problem with thing. Authoritative Salesperson (usually presented as much more intelligent than either Buyer or Best Friend) confirms discovery of Best Friend as indeed the solution to problem with thing. Buyer buys product, uses it, effortlessly solves problem with thing.

It is important to note that the product is seen as a solution to a problem with a thing. Personal relationships, happiness, love, success may be themes of the mini-drama, but they are always reduced to a problem with a thing. The thing accomplished, the love, happiness, success, or whatever, is presumed to follow naturally.

There are variations to this formula; many clever agencies even parody their own formula; some of these mini-dramas are little masterpieces of wit and visual excitement. This does not alter the basic statement which these messages make about people. The buyer is helpless, can't manage alone, suffers frustration when things (primarily) go wrong, and must purchase solutions in the form of marketed products. The salesperson, or product representative, is invariably in charge of the situation and is seen as clearly superior to the other players, who exhibit childish petulance or coy assurance. The market manager, therefore, sees the buyer as a child to be guided (at best), if not a sucker to be gulled.

These little formula dramas are seen perhaps an average of

thirty-five times each night, six to seven nights a week, forty-five or more weeks a year by an alarming plurality of American youngsters and adults.

It is very effective propaganda. It takes an existing national trait of pragmatism and sharpens it to a very narrow point indeed, transforming it to mercantile instrumentalism. Congress and government have long sought to solve our human problems with the purchase of products, as if money (our goal) was also our means: methadone as a cure for heroin addiction; helicopter gunships and sophisticated radar as a reply to guerilla fanaticism; full employment, at whatever make-work, as an answer to crime and broken families. To even dream that there is an answer in the form of a product or marketable program reveals the assumptions of propaganda: that men are mechanical dolls, that the proper key will fit their backs and make them run.

This solution-of-problem-through-product format has also been at the heart of the most popular format for television entertainment by far for the last twenty-three years: the action-adventure program. Good guys and bad guys have been bouncing around scenery for almost a quarter of a century, after cattle and gold or missile secrets and bacteriological super-poisons, with the help of six-guns or Walther PPKs, on broncos or in Mustangs. The form attained parody of itself in the sixties with James Bond as the super good guy, totally reduced to brute strength and gadget virtuosity. Not much of a success as a sleuth (he was invariably captured and tricked by the super baddies), Bond was a superb consumer of luxury products, from cars and guns to wine and women, who were themselves packaged and delivered as luxury products in this apotheosis of the pampered (and paying) consumer. Not a person or a human problem in sight. Bond's life was always saved by the proper product at the proper moment.

It is not surprising, therefore, that the treatment of ideas and events in the most mass of the media, television, and, *mutatis mutandis,* in other mass media, takes on the brevity of commercials and the closely related dramatic conflict of action-adventure. In adopting the format and methods of commercials for other kinds of programming, the media have become more dominated by the propagandizing *animus* of the modern market.

four
Mobilization Through Media

A Moog synthesizer bleeps and bloops a melodic version of the old teletype machine, making a style of urgency. Short fast cuts to location footage beat out from the tube face; the studio camera whips rapidly from one face to the other. Action News, complete with the Action News Team, is once again on the air. It is a not subtle attempt to capture the drama and tension of the action-adventure fiction film, TV's most successful format.

The rapidity and brevity of the individual stories imitate the attention-getting and non-fatiguing TV commercial format. Newsmagazines have developed a repertory of departments and a palette of sidebars and colored boxes to merchandise events and personalities in tidy and bright tidbits. It is a characteristic of the transitional media that a story of perhaps five full magazine pages is called coverage-in-depth and a series of four- or five-minute segments on television is called a mini-documentary.

The protean public is habituated to a pulsating stream of bits and pieces of information, news, advice, gossip, merchandising, warnings. There is no development, no history, no order—only the constant stream of sanitized packets. The same host will be questioning a senator for five minutes, recommending a dog food for one minute, then returning to the senator, less interested, for the final wrap-up. As a result of this kind of arrangement, this juxtaposing without articulation, viewers tend to take dog food far too seriously and senators far too casually.

Edwin Diamond, a most perceptive commentator on media behavior, has remarked that slow and steady developments which may have profound effects are not noticed by the media and thus not noticed by the public. He gives the example of the remarkable black migration to the cities of the North over a period of thirty years, with profound effects on the entire nation. Uncovered. But if there were a government official, he notes, at some point on the Mason-Dixon Line, to single out the two millionth black to cross it, and if General Motors were to award that black with a brand new Cadillac, the cameras would be there. Although Diamond does not draw this parody out, it is to be noted that what would be covered would be a self-serving ceremony for the sponsors: viewers would still be in ignorance of their condition. They would be fed just one more mental Big Mac.

With this kind of information system, it would be expected that those who wish to communicate to the public must bend themselves and their presentation to the required shape. Therefore it is a bit callous to ridicule politicians for themselves becoming actors in commercials and little "dramettes" about the "issues" the public is conditioned to expect. Just as different years of media production go through the marginal and minor cosmetic changes necessary to sustain market interest (there seems to be a three-year cycle of varying media styles and fares), so different elections have different styles of presentation. In 1976 it was sincerity and lack of big-city, high-gloss professionalism, all of which was produced with a marked degree of highly paid professionalism.

Studies indicate that people do not differentiate between news coverage of a candidate and paid political announcements about the same candidate. Although this is cited as an indication of the lack of sophistication in the viewing and listening audience, it may well be another instance of the triumph of common sense. Both the commercials and the news coverage are part of a basic system with the same motives, methods, and dynamics.

In fact, media-style commercials have become the model format for more and more areas of public discourse since the media are more and more becoming the principal, if not yet the exclusive, channels of communication between groups in America. Newsmagazine paragraphs, television interviews, full-page newspaper manifestoes, "leaked" items to news departments, documentary specials made up of bits and pieces of filmed mini-exchanges—these are the formats of conversation in our mass society. At the political conventions, covered by television, the featured events were prepared propaganda dramatizations of the *personae* of the candidates on film. The live presence of the candidates was anti-climactic and pale, after the theatre of the media-tailored message.

Although forty years ago Harold Lasswell suasively urged that communication was the essence of society, in his time he could take for granted that different agencies and methods would be used for the three principal functions of communication he delineated. Surveillance of the environment would be done by scientists, intelligence experts, astronomers, foreign travelers; peer and other interaction would take place within families, through letters, over the telephone, through legal institutions; transmission of the cultural heritage would come through clergymen, professors, parents. Since he wrote, more and more of these functions have been taken over by the media and by the marketing formats of the media. It is through the media that blacks learn about whites, the poor learn about the rich; it is the way regions learn about one another, the way parties communicate. Media channels mean media formats, and media formats mean propaganda methods. Let me cite an example.

Merchants of cigarettes want people to smoke. Commercials on television and currently in print and on billboards link the practice of smoking, through a flood of brilliant images and memorable tunes, with natural drives for security, pleasure, sex, reward, importance, even health. Public health officials, medical professionals, insurance companies, and others do not want people to smoke because smoking is associated with cancer, heart trouble, dental distress, bronchitis, ulcers, and wrinkled skin. Funds have been raised or provided through tax dollars for anti-smoking media messages. Since studies have shown that fear is an ineffective motive for changing smoking habits, the anti-smoking messages have emphasized the silliness and foolishness of smoking—its social unacceptability. These messages run directly counter to the associations established by years and years of commercials, but at least the law now prohibits television as a channel for cigarette commercials. (Since smoking appears to be an addictive drug habit for about eighty percent of nicotine users, the efficacy of anti-smoking messages is in doubt.) The point is that both cigarette manufacturers and the Public Health Service, or the American Cancer Society, look upon the public not as a group of persons with freedom, but as a market with needs and exploitable drives. Cigarette advertising is blatant propaganda. So are anti-smoking media messages. The format and the method dictate that the mentality and approach be that of propaganda. Propaganda is designed to get people to conform, to act without thinking.

It is irrelevant that abstinence from smoking is beneficial, just as not littering, contributing to the United Fund, hiring a handicapped person, not burning down national forests, going to the library, and completing school are all generally beneficial. The point is that the communication is patronizing propaganda which has become the norm for discourse. It is not a surveillance of the environment, certainly not a genuine interaction among peers, nor is it any more a transmission of heritage than a Bicentennial Minute was history. It is one interest group telling the public how to act by means of a propaganda push of a behavioral button.

Government agencies, the administrative product purchased by taxes to solve our problems with things, increasingly see their function as one of telling people what to do by means of the propaganda announcement distributed through the mass media. The Federal Energy Administration, for instance, created to help solve the problems created by the "shortage" of oil, sees its task as one of "educating" the public to conserve energy. Graphic artists and media specialists, employed by the government, archly remind us not to be "fuelish." This government "education" effort is duplicating the helpful hints of Exxon, Mobil, and Consolidated Edison, with the implied premise that the cause of the trouble is primarily in public behavior and not in government policy or corporate practice. It is a classic propaganda ploy best illustrated by parable.

There once was a careless mechanic who ruined the carburetor of an expensive car. Rather than repair the damage, he explained to the car owner that the carburetor was very delicate. He even took the trouble to write out a series of instructions that would enable the owner to drive his car despite the damage. It meant going very slowly, never shifting above second gear, idling at least ten minutes before moving out, never using the air conditioning. After the initial shock, the owner was mildly grateful to the mechanic for his obvious solicitude and expert advice.

The point of the parable is that we have come full circle in the reduction of virtually every experience to a problem in principle soluble through the purchase of a product. Once the product, in this case a government agency, is in place, it finds things more intractable than the unorganized public. The public is then reduced to the impersonal status of thing, and held responsible for the problem. If the agency fails to solve the problem, it cannot be blamed. The public, the purchasers of the product through taxes, *are* the problem.

Government agencies, educational institutions, marketing corporations, all use the media and all show the instrumental assumptions of the propagandizing mentality: truth is whatever is said effectively; morality is the assigning of responsibility to others; aesthetics are useful for packaging. These conditions have created a very special kind of technical and bureaucratic bedlam.

With reporters and interviewers trying to connect their particular assignment to topics in demand by editors (the so-called issues), and with authors, politicians, government spokesmen, show business agents, corporate flacks, actors, doctors—all the people in the news who wish publicity to sell a product or who seek to avoid criticism for themselves or their employers, trying to give responses and replies that will achieve their own particular propagandistic purpose—the result is a true dialogue of the deaf. Each side of the exchange seeks to use the other to reach an unseen and unheard audience—the public. The public itself is dispersed and at the receiving end of instruments that cannot carry back any kind of response to the dialogue-pretenders before camera or microphone or reporter's notepad. Yet these exchanges are being multiplied by the thousand to produce material for news departments and to create demand for information packages, to stimulate desired activity among people whether it be voting or buying pornography.

This playing to the unseen and imagined crowd with a routine repertoire of tested issues and acceptable attitudes gives a strange and alienated air to press conferences, interviews, speeches, and all occasions of media-distributed discourse. The participants have a harried air of perpetual distraction, as if there were a time lapse between utterance and acknowledgment, as if they were humming tunes they cannot quite hear themselves, as if their native language were not being used. The best image for this condition of our national substitute for conversation is of a roving reporter on the floor of a political convention. There is a milling crowd within which he can be picked out by the little "hearing aid" that connects him with the program director. He is looking frantically for a person-in-the-news as the non-celebrated in the mob stroke the hem of his garment. When he does find one, they both squint uncertainly in the direction of the long-lensed camera. After the reporter has asked a question designed to provoke a stock response suiting the script the personage has been assigned by the media, he touches his ear and frowns in concentration, trying to listen to directions from his TV boss as the personage drones on, unattended by his questioner. The noise from the mouth stops. Both smile. Roving reporter takes up whole picture and wraps up in thirty seconds what he knew the personage was supposed to say according to his and general editorial expectations. Throughout, there has been the din of the crowd and the flashing of lights. This real scene is an allegory for the forum of transitional public opinion, peopled by programmed puppets, engulfed in propaganda.

five
Dictating Demand

The eighteenth-century gentlemen who debated and adopted the First Amendment felt that, in the absence of restrictions on free speech or the press, open discussion of policies and issues would occur automatically and there would be a healthy and diverse electorate. Mill of course saw that social pressures and the tyranny of the majority could stifle a fresh thought, for it would shut a shy mouth. Neither could have foreseen the growing demand for what is called access (to the media) as a right connected with freedom of expression. They could not have foreseen the technical complexity and enormous capital costs required to maintain media systems.

Groups and individuals are demanding access because the media are the sole means by which Americans can talk to one another in any realistically significant way. Those who demand access cannot afford the high cost of renting the media machine and the even higher cost of engaging professional sophists of the technology software, who know how to translate (and necessarily transform) ideas, plans, and programs into the media language of bits and pieces of dramatized propaganda.

The inaccessibility of the media to the private citizen without a large fortune no doubt is the prime psychological cause of the growing feeling of helplessness in the face of complex and vexing problems of technical dimensions unforeseen by the eighteenth-century authors of the First Amendment. Yet this inaccessibility and consequent frustration of citizens who feel they don't count (and who are less inclined to vote than any of their European counterparts who are enfranchised), exist at a time when, paradoxically, media managers are trying to discover the opinions of the masses and of specific segments among the masses as frantically as the managers of other mass-market enterprises are trying to discover the buying preferences of their customers. With all the interest in the opinion of the public, with all the publications of facts and figures and samples of actual individual opinion among the masses, with television reporters going into the streets and asking anonymous citizens what they think for frequently national distribution, and always for a sizable audience at least—with all this, why do people feel that their opinions do not count? They certainly are measured.

Just as the marketing system of the media sets up certain internal necessities that give a propagandistic twist to all their communications from the few senders to the many receivers, so too these same necessities work on the systems that are used to discover and report on the opinions and feeling of the public.

First of all, the overwhelming bulk of opinion solicitation is connected with product promotion, not with public policy nor with any ideas of non-commercial import. Most of the questions asked by corporations and by government deal with preferences for things, or dissatisfaction with things. Since this kind of solicitation is the best financed, the other kinds get less imaginative and technical resources allotted to them, and their methods tend to imitate the preponderant formats, with their built-in biases, for product promotion.

Secondly, opinion solicitation and subsequent measurement are primarily business operations that must show a profit. Quality and accuracy are expensive. Pollsters, as they are aptly termed in Timese, are basically businessmen. In order to be successful, the opinion business must keep simple and please its buyers. The buyers are never disinterested in the results. They are politicians, news business managers, federal agencies. Each has internal purposes that dictate policy.

Significantly, the opinions are *solicited.* They are not listened to as one would test the content of a river by dipping into the waters and drawing out a sample. Opinions are attitudes that are sharpened to statements about specific events, persons, places, programs, problems, questions. The people who control discussion, information, and news are basically the same people who are asking the questions. To select from the thousands of possible topics, to formulate specific questions from billions of possible forms and formats, to be predisposed toward marketing methods, is to predetermine the conclusion and the shape of the solicited opinion.

Finally, and most importantly, opinion surveys are founded on transactions that are the polar opposites of the proper setting for the exchange of ideas and the building up of the individual cells necessary for the formation of a genuine public opinion about an issue. In the traditional forum, members of a given public know one another; the public is simply the larger aggregate of a number of primary groups or small face-to-face gatherings. Discussion among these groups is frank and full; strong members influence weak ones. The view of the whole is different from the view of the individuals. The exchanges are in natural settings; they come about spontaneously. When a definite decision has to be reached, meetings may be called that are more formal and a definite vote can be taken.

To know someone's opinions, one must know the person, his character, and his history. One must at least spend a few relaxed hours with him as his guest, to get some idea of the shape of his thoughts. And it is an exchange. He in turn must get to know his interrogator. Before summitry, when diplomats had a task to perform, their job largely consisted of getting to know the leadership of a country and translating, as well as transmitting that knowledge to their own leadership. It involved hours and years of socializing, not questionnaires.

Scientific polling methods are to public opinion what artificial insemination is to human love-making. Unlike artificial insemination, however, polling is sterile. Surveys proceed among strangers. The public whose varying numerical percentages are soberly reported as holding this or that opinion is an abstract extrapolation from an aggregate of strangers, interviewed by strangers according to a carefully prepared format or script. In fact, any deviation from the script, any accidental meeting of friends in an interview will disturb the scientific validity of the exchange as an atomistic ingredient in a carefully concocted piece of research.

Critics of polls often point out how carelessly some polls are done—that college students or housewives are hired for low pay off the street, given a phone book and a schedule of questions, or an address list, and carfare, and told to go out and collect opinions. They cheat, of course. They fill out responses themselves, they go to the wrong addresses, they don't know how to take accurate notes, they get into arguments with their respondents. This does happen and it happens far more frequently than pollsters or their customers would want to admit. But it is not failure to follow proper procedure that makes opinion surveys unreliable. It is the proper procedure, with its assumption of people as atoms and questions as neutral probes, that has substituted an elaborate fiction for public opinion.

A stranger can ask another stranger, in the appropriate impersonal setting, what toothpaste he uses. But, as tests have shown, such apparently innocent questions as "Do you have a library card?" produce a raft of simple falsehoods. So even simple questions of fact or of product preferences in areas that do not very deeply involve the total person frequently come up with the wrong answer or with none at all.

Vast experience with asking questions in sterile settings has given polling organizations sophistication in asking further questions in sterile settings. People may lie when asked certain types of questions. If one asks a drunk if he is married (in a survey of alcoholics and degenerates), he will say no, since he is ashamed of his failure to maintain his marriage. So, to foil this predicted ploy of the respondent, one asks, "Where is your wife?" Some will pretend to have voted when in fact they have not, so they are asked where one registers to vote in a given district. These questions are of course mere demographic questions—means to locate the respondent on a grid of characteristics, not to find out what is on his mind.

There are instances of the so-called open-ended interview, where the interviewer is rather sophisticated and quite a long time has been allotted for the exchange, perhaps as much as four or five hours. But, of course, at the end of such an interview the record of the interviewee's opinions must be analyzed, coded, and compared with other open-ended interviews. The problem with the open-ended interview is that it is too good to be useful, too complete to be reduced to a graph, too nuanced to be made into a unit of measurement.

In every procedure for the measurement and reporting of public opinion, technicians intervene and apply techniques of easily repeatable reduction in order to organize the data into more manipulable form. This is perhaps why the most popular methods begin with a reductive technique: the Likert scale, or simple true/false items, or more ingenious and thus more intrusive techniques such as the quintamensional format for schedule items. The instrument for soliciting opinions more and more resembles an objective exam given in high school by a teacher infatuated with "trick" questions and alienated from his subject and his students.

Finally, of course, the opinions solicited among the public must be reported to the buyer of the survey, who then uses it for his purposes, which may be to buttress a previously chosen position, to impress a client, to provide a pretext for an editorial, or to prepare the groundwork for a campaign to sell soap, a candidate, or an unpopular war.

Whether the reductive techniques intervene early or late in the procedures, they will in the end have presented statements and answers to prepared questions as a series of numbers. The numbers are presumed to have comparability of significance. Thus, it is not uncommon to compare the "popularity rating" of different presidents at different times during their own administrations and those of others. Pundits will draw meaning from these comparisons, as if 42 percent of a group of 1962 Americans responding to a particular question at a certain point in history could be univocally compared to 58 percent of 1975 Americans responding to a similar—but only similar—question at another point in history, which includes consciousness of the 1962 moment. Identical units can be put on the same scale. But if a pound of sugar is quite a different matter from a pound of tobacco, or mountain air, or rock salt, or Shylock's flesh, then surely a percentage point of one group's opinion is not even a percentage of something, but rather of an abstraction of an extrapolation of a projection.

One of the best surveys ever taken of a national sample was done in 1964 by Hadley Cantril and Lloyd Free, both gifted technicians of the science and art of constructing opinion surveys. The results were published in book form, appropriately titled *The Political Beliefs of Americans.* It is a masterpiece of clarity of conception, authority of execution, and of cautious modesty in its conclusions.

The survey, which was expensive because its sample was so carefully drawn and fully solicited with a complicated and lengthy schedule of questions over a period of time, was intended to simplify and clarify the distinction between liberal and conservative. There was an attempt made to scientifically characterize the American public in terms of this classic dichotomy of political analysis. Cantril and Free were not mere head counters. In a literate and witty chapter, they detailed the history of the terms "liberal" and "conservative" and pointed out how dreadfully confusing these terms were in recent history alone, to say nothing of the last two hundred years. Such a rich texture of historical meaning is unsuitable to survey research, they frankly admitted. The terms must be reduced to something operational, to concepts that can be related to concrete actions of readily identifiable type. For the purposes of their survey, therefore, they defined liberalism as the view that the Federal government should intervene in local matters and in general expand its powers in order to meet social needs. Conservatism would be the diametrically opposite viewpoint. Beyond these operational definitions, the authors indicated that there does lie what they called an ideological spectrum. The liberal view is based on the "ideology" that people are good and deserving of aid. The conservative view is based on the "ideology" that individuals differ, and that individual effort should be rewarded, while individual failure should be accepted without government interfering in a natural process.

Cantril and Free then asked thousands of questions which broke up these basic and simple ideas (carefully constructed to be basic and simple) into questions related to possible actions, e.g., "Should the Federal government help pay teachers' salaries?"—or to simple circumstances, e.g., "Is financial success due primarily to hard work or good luck?"

There is something admirable and refreshing in any effort to ground grandiose phrases on concrete pedestrian instances. It is better to ask someone how many hours a day he spends in silent prayer than to ask if he believes in a contemplative dimension to human fulfillment. At least in a certain sense it is. But if there is no sensitivity to nuance, to individual differences, the question is too reductive, as if one were to prove or disprove the presence of gourmet taste by weighing the amount of food consumed weekly by subjects.

After all their effort, Cantril and Free came up with the not startling conclusion that Americans were "operationally liberal" and "ideologically conservative." Translated back into the pedestrian items they used to construct these relatively

grand abstractions of their own, this apparent paradox is re-
solved. The survey merely found out that the majority of
Americans want all the help and money they can get from the
government, but they do not want to pay more taxes and they
do not want to be told how to live or how to spend their money
by the government in Washington.

Along the way to establishing this characterization of Americans, Cantril and Free correlated these traits of conservatism
and liberalism with other traits which they defined by means of
simple questions. One of these traits was optimism/pessimism.

Respondents were shown a diagram that was called a "ladder
of happiness" with ten steps. The bottom step would represent
a very wretched and miserable condition. The top step repre-
sented total bliss. "Now, where do you suppose you are now on
this ladder? Thank you. Now would you mind guessing where
you will be on this ladder, say, five years from now? Thank
you."

As might be supposed, most people placed themselves a bit
above the midpoint of happiness for the present, and an addi-
tional bit above that point for the future. Operational conserva-
tives, however, tended to see themselves going up less than one
rung in the future. Of course, they found themselves a bit higher
on the ladder for the moment than most people.

It is easy to deride this kind of game, but it is played in deadly
earnest, and it also is able to measure some truths about the
manners and social habits of Americans, if not about their
inmost feelings about the country and about themselves.

The Cantril-Free study, merely because it was survey research, had to ignore history and individual differences in order
to come up with data that would fit the grid of a report. While
compelled to reduce developed and nuanced concepts, with
historical meaning, to operational bases for simple questions,
the researchers were also constrained to concoct new abstractions to summarize the answers to these simple questions.
"Predominantly liberal" is a phrase that would naturally evoke

some historic connotations in a conversation; in a report it must be restricted to mean a definite group of respondents who responded in a definite pattern to certain simple questions.

Robert Penn Warren said in 1974 that "the ideal of studying men and telling their story, noble or vicious, will be replaced by the study of statistics or nonideographic units of an infinite series." These units, he added, may be breathing, but they will not be selves. " . . . if there is no past, there can be no self."

The opinion survey is the instrument that reduces both men and ideas to units, to interchangeable parts. It must reduce ideas to operational concepts for the formulation of questions. It must reduce men to responding units that can be grouped into types, statistical types. It destroys the self, it does away with history. It is thus an integral part of the transitional forum of public opinion, managed by the mass marketing techniques of the news and information business.

The Cantril-Free study was done more than a decade ago. It was done superbly well; it was not done for any directly commercial purpose. Since then more sophisticated techniques have been devised with regard to the details of polling, particularly the use of the focus group. The focus group is a small primary group of people selected by a variety of methods from the population under study. They are presented with topics related to the matter that will be used in the later survey. Their discussion is observed by social scientists either directly or through closed-circuit television or one-way mirrors (a device more useful in impressing the client who is paying for the service with his power and importance than in ensuring "objectivity" among the participants). The discussion is examined to pick out central themes that may well serve as focal points around which to construct questions, or items, on the schedule, or questionnaire. This, and other later techniques, only intensify the nature of the poll as the symmetric complement to the mass media management of messages as items for sale and behavioral stimuli to action.

Never before have so many powerful organizations and groups, and the government itself, shown such interest in private views and opinions, and yet never before have people felt so ignored and arrogantly put upon. Inmost thoughts and attitudes, of course, are of no interest to pollsters and their customers. It is future actions that they care about—votes, investments, purchases. Thus, individuals are programmed to answer scientifically concocted promptings designed to elicit only useful information—useful from the point of view of the poll purchaser. Thus human beings are assigned the role of respondent, as they have been assigned the roles of viewer, reader, listener, consumer. All the roles share the note of passivity in the face of bland management. Respondents are not individuals with opinions; they are predictable types who have been examined for predictable types of response.

In the same way, the revelations about FBI and CIA invasions of privacy are outrageous for deeper reasons than their violation of civil rights. It is their instrumental attitude toward thought. These agencies could not care less what ideas their suspects have except insofar as they are clues to action, action that the police wish to predict, and thus prevent. Thus, from a functional point of view, the readership profiles, voting patterns, and market surveys sold to mass marketers are the same instruments as police files on subversive groups. The only difference, judging from revelations about FBI files, is that the police files are constructed with considerably less skill and imagination. As a result, markets are managed with greater efficiency than law is ordered.

The transitional forum of public opinion is of remarkable coherence. A variety of causes have collaborated to produce the transformation of the forum. Mill's ideal traditional forum for public opinion was peopled by free, rational, particular individuals who engaged in debate within a commonly accepted universe of discourse toward the realization of moral values through public policies.

American assumptions of instrumentalism, the mechanisms of mass marketing, the economic necessities of the news and information business, the multi-cultural awareness of internationalism, the vast complexities of high technology have created the transitional forum. Free individuals are being replaced by predictable types, publics are becoming audiences, issues are assigned topics for harmless comment. The will of the people is now the mood of the mass; methods of communications are subverted to techniques of propaganda.

six
Celebrating
Authority

Central to the notion of freedom of expression as a social necessity for the growth of groups as well as individuals is the concept of authority which is its complement. For Mill there were two kinds of authority. The first is the authority of government. This authority he stipulated as stemming from a tacit agreement between the governed and the governors based on regrettable necessity. Someone must be in charge of the arrangements, must determine traffic, must arbitrate disputes. In common with the Founding Fathers of the American republic, he felt that this necessary power of government had a tendency to grow and increase. Free men must ever keep it in check, and therefore they must keep it in mind. With mere anarchy, there would be no practical freedom. This was the original notion behind the Federal Radio Commission, the ancestor of the Federal Communications Commission. Some arbiter must assign broadcast frequencies or the airwaves would be jammed with simultaneous signals, and no one would be heard.

The second kind of authority was the more important. It was the sovereignty of reason. Reason was the organ of truth. All men bowed to logic, ultimately. If belief inspired passion, disinterested search for the truth was a pure passion. Although astutely aware that each age had its prejudices (one of his strong reasons for allowing the greatest possible freedom of discussion and dissent), Mill shared many of the common assumptions of his day. Among them were belief in the supremacy of reason and identification of reason with the cultivated form it took in European civilized discourse of the period. Despite the gulf of language and sensibilities between them, Mill would have recognized Berelson's ideal democratic citizen as a man of reason and cultivated sense.

The sovereignty of reason confers authority on the man of knowledge and the man of wisdom. Ideally, the myth of leadership sees the executive as a man of wisdom, aided by experts, men of knowledge. The man of knowledge and the man of wisdom can only be recognized for what they are in a universe of discourse that has standards: standards of logic, standards of factual accuracy, rules of evidence, and accepted moral principles. Within this context men listen to reason. Democratic leadership derives its authority from its respect for reason and reasons urged by responsible spokesmen, as broadcast editorials phrase it.

But when there is no cultural confidence, when there is no agreement about the nature, let alone the sovereignty, of reason, there can be no authority accorded to men of knowledge and men of wisdom. In a transitional period, authority is merely stipulated to exist in the credentialed—the advanced-degree holders, the officers of trust, the owners of resources. Enthusiasm about "the knowledge society" notwithstanding, it is not knowledge that is respected, but the vestigial signs of cultural esteem. As time goes on, this esteem, since it is without substantive foundation, turns into contempt. Thus, demand for increased distribution of college degrees and professional diplomas among disadvantaged groups is being followed, with embarrassing rapidity, by disillusionment with the power and economic value of advanced education. Even the meaning of the term "knowledge" changes. It begins to mean access to hidden facts and procedures whose existence affects the making and losing of money. Men of knowledge are replaced by men in the know.

Leaders find wisdom in consulting polls, devised by pollsters, to determine what the most popular view of the moment is and to act in such manner as not to offend this popular view. The lack of cultural confidence that leads to distrust of former standards as measures of truth sends governors and governed to polls as new sources of authority. The mechanistic reduction-isms inevitable in the polling procedures are ignored. It is the safest way to decide on how to package treatment of public questions, whatever may be done about them. The action taken by officials is dictated by immediate norms of expediency, since there is no agreement about moral principles except in terms of rhetoric.

The traditional forum also was determined by majority de-cree, but in a different manner. The standards were sovereign and they were perceived and used by reason. But the standards and the reason were, of course, culturally conditioned, which is to say they had a long history of development among certain peoples living in certain climates. Over centuries, certain prac-tices changed and certain principles emerged. What survived was what the majority of generations approved and handed on.

The vast majority of the dead outweighed the minority of the living. Now, of course, in our transitional forum, the vast ma-jority of the living outweigh the minority of the dead. The population explosion has, one might say, its spiritual dimen-sion. It is a commonplace that 95 percent of all the scientists who ever lived are alive today. True, but 50 percent of all the psychopathic killers who ever lived are alive today. We also have a majority of rapists and poets, garbage collectors and philosophers, lunatics and lovers. With each passing day, the living increase their numerical strength over the dead, and thus, in a strange way, their authority—the authority of overwhelm-ing numbers.

In numbers there are sales and therefore strength. The same

marketing mechanisms that meet the economic needs of media management are also operative in the collection (through polls) and distribution (through the mass media) of opinion. There is simply no time for the living to communicate well-thought-out positions to one another, as the dead have done through their patiently accumulated opinions enshrined in the legitimacy of institutions and customs, many of which cannot cope with the sheer necessity for arranging affairs in ever greater complexity under more globally and psychologically crowded conditions.

The sheer weight and presence of collected and distributed opinion creates trends and climates of opinion; these vague feelings for what most people seem to want or think are crystallized into packaged issues by pollsters and news business managers. Since politicians, public officials, clergymen and pundits must seek some common ground with the faceless hordes who are their clients, they must address themselves and their resources to these issues and topics.

Thus both the authority found in government as a regrettable necessity and the authority conferred on knowledgeable experts and wise executives by performance and achievement according to set standards are sucked dry of any living force and are replaced by the authority, anonymous and vague, of the lowest common denominator of the marketplace. In this type of transitional forum, political leaders are relegated to the role of managers of the inevitable. Scientific expertise is for sale to the controlling private interests of the marketplace—as in energy, transportation, agriculture, defense, and communications. Just as the nature of the media intensifies the natural systematic effect of high technology, so also does the nature of the media intensify and hasten this transformation of the nature of authority.

Writing, the printing press, high-speed rotary presses, the telegraph, the telephone, radio, television—each succeeding medium makes it easier for a single source to reach more people with more information. The presence of space satellites has equalized the reach of virtually all the employed bands of the electromagnetic spectrum.

Early media tend to place high skill demands on the user and thus limit the number of messages to those of reasonable quality and of some importance (to the user). Later media place little skill demand on the actual user (as opposed to the operator, increasingly relegated to a janitorial function removed from the user and the content of the message). Access to the media is thus determined primarily by money, not by specialized skill. Authority is conferred on what is transmitted because it is transmitted. This is the basic law of communications economics that makes Boorstin's observation about celebrities—people well known for their well-known qualities—a systematic necessity. In the realm of the opinion of the marketplace and the authority of the marketplace, the television commentator, who is paid to issue his opinions through the most market-dominated medium, is the best personification. As Nicholas Von Hoffman has noted, television commentators live in celebrated obscurity. Everyone knows who they are but no one can remember a thing they ever said. Voltaire would be too offensive to minority groups and the establishment, Samuel Johnson would be too untelegenic and gross to get a job on a network. Nor would either consent to being turned on and off like light bulbs.

Generally speaking, less expert people have more access to more effective media of communication as the technologies improve. Few people write books (few people read them). More people write letters. Still more people make telephone calls. Compare the quality of discourse (on the average) of a university lecture with the quality of discourse on a television talk show (also on the average). Compare the general level of intelligence exhibited in a radio interview with a public personality to the level of intelligence revealed in a radio program which answers phone calls on the air.

Since there are no standards of knowledge or wisdom required for access to the media, but rather standards of market value—either one can buy space and time, or one can merit enough market interest to attract advertising support—it is no wonder that the demand for access among the disadvantaged or the disenfranchised does not refer to the quality or level or importance of their message, but merely to the fact that they are not heard and thus are not treated fairly. If there are sufficient numbers within a group, they may well be granted the time by a local station. The criterion is the authority of the market or the allied criterion of numerical strength.

The Public Broadcasting System is no exception to this rule. The use of a capital-intensive medium requires heavy financing and financing must follow marketing rules and the rule of numbers. Either foundations and corporations or tax monies are the prime source of funding for public television. To get repeated funding, the programs must attract sufficient numbers to please the financier. This is the explanation for the increasingly strident use of advertising and promotion by public television as a system and by local public stations. The more corporate support is given, the more the programs will resemble their commercial counterparts in both programming and advertising for patronage of the programming. The more taxpayer support is given, the more programming will be influenced by ruling parties and their constituencies. Audience-supported programs are rare and the level of support does not permit the most effective use of the medium.

When we leave the realm of broadcasting, with the legal strictures imposed by the FCC and the public policy of promoting diversity, the level and quality of discourse and opinion are virtually in the exclusive dominion of market forces. Letters-to-the-editor columns and their expanded cousin, the Op-Ed page, are under the exclusive control of the paper or magazine in which they appear.

Opinions, then, derive authority not from some standard of reason but from the mere fact of their currency. Only this bizarre, yet commonplace, truth about our times can make sense of the practice (absurd, by reasonable standards in a universe where truth is sought) of the endorsement by a celebrity of a product or an idea or even an ideal, as a means to sales, acceptance or devotion. If a celebrity is a celebrity because he is celebrated, an opinion is persuasive, an idea is important, an ideal is worthy because it is endorsed by a celebrity. In a way, the celebrity invests the things related to him with, not surprisingly, celebrity. In the market-dominated transitional forum, this is authority.

Thus comedians have successfully urged the public to support research to cure diseases. Nobel Prize winners in the very area of research that requires support would not do as well as the comedian. Actors have gotten votes for politicians. Famous athletes have overcome male prejudice against cosmetics and scents. Olympic stars sell sports clothes. Movie actresses lend support to abortion-on-demand campaigns. Shakespearean actors of international reputation sell cameras. To complete the circle, Nobel Prize winners in physics and biology have donned the mantle of social and political wisdom and urged doubtful public policies.

To produce a movie, get a star. To cure diseases, get a star. To sell soap, get a star. To save souls, get a star. To be heard, be a star.

With the exception of so-called public service, all of these endorsements are bought and paid for. The public service endorsements give the star increased exposure and celebrity, which will increase his or her price for the next commercial endorsement or performance.

If a cause or a charity receives notice, and thus worthiness, by association with a celebrity, the celebrity acquires a patina of serious purpose and the image of depth from his or her association with the cause or charity. Functionally speaking, Joan Baez and Bob Hope have followed the same path of allying their public performances with political causes and, in the process, identifying their particular styles of entertainment with definite political attitudes. As a result, matching the parity on television of politician and product, senators and dog food, the nation tends to take performers too seriously and public policies too casually, as if debate were a form of highly paid entertainment. In refusing to accept the Academy Award and sending an Indian in his place to make a political speech (unscheduled and unanticipated), Marlon Brando had merely exploited a national assumption: celebrity is authority.

An economic necessity for mass media management, the star syndrome has become an obsession outside of media circles. Schools, clubs, churches—any institutions involved in gathering people together for a purpose—are now immersed in competition for stars as attractions. The first consideration is not who is knowledgeable about a subject or project; it is rather who is known and can thus publicize the given interest. The original purpose is lost in the scramble to touch celebrity and bask in its glow.

One of the greatest celebrities of all time was Richard Nixon. Presidents, with their personal planes, helicopters, ceremonies of state and great power, make good pictures and good copy. Nixon, who had lost the close election of 1960 to a master of star glamor, John F. Kennedy, was not about to repeat his mistakes. He spent an inordinate amount of time brooding over his image; hired the very best technicians and media specialists to enhance his stardom; made his visit to China an international media event, with a new satellite fired into synchronous orbit just in time to provide high quality color television, live, from the Great Wall to Peoria.

Malcolm Muggeridge has written that the press follow the great the way sharks follow ocean liners in the hope that someone will fall off and provide a rich feast of copy. Nixon's fall, of course, provided one of the richest feasts of copy in history. No greater evidence can be garnered for the maxim that celebrity is authority.

All the henchmen of Nixon, including the convicted con-
spirators, were spectacularly in demand by the media, and their
words and images have been handsomely paid for. The amount
of attention paid by the media to the policies and activities of
the Nixon administration in domestic and foreign affairs is cast
into dim shadow by the quantity and stridency of coverage of
palace intrigues, Washington gossip, and personality sketches
of the celebrities of shame he created.

Woodward and Bernstein of the *Washington Post,* the two
reporters most instrumental in bringing the Watergate scandals
to light, wrote a best-selling book about their disclosures. The
book has been made into a blockbuster movie, with two guaranteed moneymaking stars playing the parts of Woodward and
Bernstein. At the premiere of the film in Washington, D.C.,
fans and admirers mobbed the two stars; Woodward and Bernstein were present but comparatively unnoticed.

The demand for access to the media forum is thus far deeper
than the age-old desire of all men for their day in court. It is
the realization that recognition by the media opens the door to
celebration by the media—the fountainhead of authority and
thus of legitimacy in a society that has lost its traditional moor-
ings and the attendant standards of both political and expert
authority.

Terrorists have multiplied in this new arena of authority-
through-celebrity. Merely by attracting the attention of the
media, terrorists know that their cause will achieve some measure of legitimacy it did not have before. The media will make
them and their cause "real." The desperately craved public
attention that has become almost a solitary source of significance can more than compensate some hostages for the danger
to their lives. Hostages in Sweden, Brooklyn, and France have
become friends and admirers of their former captors.

Early in 1976 Dick Cavett, a television "host" and professional comedy writer, was the organizing personality of a television special about film. Just before the closing credits, Cavett

walked slowly forward along a street of a major Hollywood studio back lot—the shrine of vast props and sets from great films of the past. Earnestly looking into the lens, Cavett recalled his boyhood of Saturday afternoon filmviewing in the small town of Nebraska where he grew up dreaming of New York and Hollywood and the great places of the great world, images of which were brought to him exclusively by the silver screen. With emotion he recalled the great films he had seen and asked the rhetorical question, "Which is the real world, which is more real, the world inside the screen, or the world outside the screen?" Two years before that an old poet from the South ventured to his audience: ". . . the post-Cartesian nightmare of the unreality of the world and the self would be converted by a benign dramaturgy into a continuous daydream so expertly staged, lighted, and directed, that it becomes real."

In the transitional forum of packaged issues and star endorsements, where publics have become audiences, opinions are not so much held because of the reasons or insights that support them as they are cherished for the commonality they give the opinion holder with the celebrity who is identified with them. Differences of opinion are not so much matters of debate as dramatic conflicts of taste and class—differences subject not so much to rational judgment as to preference and purchasing power. The casting of a vote thus becomes more an expression of style than an act of conviction. The paradoxical consequence is that mere preference is often held with a tenacity and rigidity that rivals Puritan conformity, because the preference is a fragile source of identity in an agoraphobic society.

seven

Manipulation and Membership

In what seems to have been an unwitting parallel of Lasswell's three social functions of communications, the famous Smith-Bruner-White study, *Opinions and Personality,* summed up the authors' conceptual understanding of the relationship between individuals and the ideas that they espoused in three functions: object appraisal, social adjustment, externalization.

By the phrase "object appraisal" the study means simply knowledge—but in the context of ego defense. For Lasswell, the first function of communication was the surveillance of the environment to keep the members of a society safe from external harm or internal decay. Echoing this homely truth, Av Westin, former head of ABC Television News, has pointed out that the first thing people want to learn from news broadcasts is that they and their families are at least safe for one more night. Then they want to learn if anyone else may have been devoured by external evil or internal rot. Then they may be interested in any signs of future danger. Long-term trends (as news, or as knowledge for self-defense) put them to sleep.

Opinions, therefore, do primarily serve what Daniel Katz has called (but ill-defined) the knowledge function. Paradoxically, opinions help us to know by substituting for knowledge, by being necessary but poor replacements for knowledge. There are opinions about whether there is intelligent life on other planets. There are opinions about whether a personal God exists. If God appears in the sky or little green men land on Long Island, opinions will be superseded by knowledge.

As substitutes for knowledge, opinions act as presuppositions and informal hypotheses that help us to arrive at certainty. "It's a bird, it's a plane! No! It's Superman!" This familiar pop-culture formula is just one more instance of what anyone does whenever he looks out the window, scans an x-ray, reads an auditor's report, or takes someone new out to dinner. Opinions provide a framework within which to ask questions. They organize experience and structure expectations. They are provisional, but necessary, substitutes for knowledge.

Stereotypes, in this context, are opinions which have become permanent, rather than provisional, substitutes for knowledge. They act as a barrier against future experience and the assimilation of new evidence. They are fixed and rigid. Being fixed and permanent, stereotypical opinions militate against the knowledge function, which is dynamic and adaptive. Since some opinions are indeed stereotypical, there is every indication that opinions do a lot more than merely help us to know about the world around us.

For Lasswell, too, communication in society did not confine itself to the mundane task of looking for wolves on the horizon. James Carey has pointed out that McLuhan saw the media of communications as ways of structuring our experience, whereas the other and deeper Canadian analyst of communications, Harold Adams Innis, saw the media as institutions within society that structured social organization. Lasswell was like Innis in this respect. He saw communications in the socially organized form of institutions: the legislature, the executive, the judiciary, the churches, the clubs, the army. And he saw communications as the social function which made it possible for these disparate parts to perform their separate functions and coordinated them to enable the organism of the whole to live. Very much a body politic, very much akin to St. Paul's notion of the body mystical, society was alive.

The social adjustment function of the Smith-Bruner-White study parallels the social interaction function of Lasswell, but in the microcosm of the personal world of individual relationships. At this level, and from this viewpoint, communication is looked upon as a sort of money, a medium of exchange, whose units of currency are opinions—the content of the things we say to one another that are not mere announcements of fact. Conversations are exchanges of this mental money in transactions that bind individuals together or keep them apart as leader and led, lover and beloved, parent and child, friends or enemies, partners or rivals. This function of opinion is entirely social and is seen most clearly in the myriad personal judgments that are exchanged in elevators, restaurants, shops, factories and offices about the present state and probable future of the weather. It is because outer weather, as Robert Frost has made explicit, is such a marvelously apt metaphor for inner weather, that opinions about the weather are so valuable to social adjustment. It enables one to be clearly but not offensively friendly or remote, to indicate feelings about life or about the moment—to communicate or withhold inner states. Even farmers, fishermen, and pilots, whose lives and livelihood depend on real knowledge about outer weather, use opinions about weather far more for personal social adjustment.

In *The Four Loves,* C. S. Lewis indicates that friendship (one of the four along with affection, eros, and charity) cannot exist without some third object—a common bond or interest or membership—that is the necessary atmosphere within which friendship can breathe and grow. Friendship would be destroyed by constant declarations of mutual esteem which were not *about* anything—whether boating, or golf, or literature, or films, or flowers, or paintings.

Shared sensibility seems to be the *sine qua non* of friendship.

Shared sensibility seems to survive differences of view about the meaning of life, about religion, politics, sexual orientation, or occupational values. Two men can be ardent Presbyterians, Democrats, from the same town, with the same income, but their potential relationship might well be shattered if one were to play his favorite bird calls and the other collapsed into derisory laughter at the fearful racket birds make. Friends must share sensibility and they must share sensibility about something.

Some opinions, therefore, are necessary for us to herald the kind of sensibility we have to offer. In this nation of strangers, who send signals to one another by the goods they own and by the cut of their hair as well as of their clothes, opinions about media subjects become codes for inner weather. It is significant that political and even philosophical conversations in the present U.S.A. are considered most satisfying if they show where someone's "head is at." The discussion—and public opinion is made up of countless personal discussions—is not so much about a subject for mutual learning about the world as it is an occasion to reveal sensibilities, to declare the group identified with, and to invite or reject auditors on the basis of this imputed sensibility. The group identified with may not even exist, in the sense that the Salvation Army and the Teamsters Union both exist. People may wish to show they are Northeastern Intellectuals or Swingers or Independent Radicals or Conservative Republicans or Rich as Hell. Private talk, in effect, begins to imitate public talk, the political interviews and celebrity exposure of the media, which are trying to capture the informal spontaneity of natural personal interchange. Life imitates artifice.

The knowledge function and the social adjustment function are not necessarily mutually exclusive. A psychiatrist can give his colleagues a brilliant opinion about a case, knowing it will enhance his reputation for wit and elegance, as well as for professional insight. He also knows it will help the patient to get better when used in treatment. A Supreme Court Justice can write a determinative decision in such a way that he will be admired by the group he seeks to align himself with and will also serve justice.

Often, however, the social adjustment function rigidifies an opinion into a stereotype. Individuals fear that change or truth might disturb their alliances or compromises or illusions. The stereotype tells them what they want, rather than what is. As a counter in mental money, it props up a transaction that both parties feel is more necessary or desirable than any learning of a new fact or truth.

More and more, the opinions people use to understand the world come from the mass media. As we have seen, the mass media are predominantly marketing, rather than informational, media. The information and news that they distribute is already packaged for consumption in the form of an issue, tailored and targeted for sensibilities and tendencies already researched. The pressures of time and money further ensure the efficacy of the overwhelming pressures for stereotyping.

The sale of products is geared to appeal to the customers' longing for social acceptance and group membership. Therefore consumers of a given mass-produced and mass-distributed product become members of what Boorstin has termed "consumer communities." Advertising is very explicit about this: That Cosmopolitan Girl; The Pepsi Generation; The Marlboro Man. Consumption of a product is a declaration of identity.

The commercial setting for news and information and public affairs tends to make of opinions themselves one more product. To espouse an opinion, therefore, is to join a group. But the group may be a ghost, as the creation of consumer publics is the figment of advertising copywriters. However, in a world where to say is to know and to be known is to be authorized, the mere declaration of a group's existence may call it into being—at least as a force to deal with in further media discussions. Nixon's media team were masters of this technique, having created The Silent Majority, a group all the more present by its absence. To be in favor of Nixon was not so attractive a concept as to be included in a secret, yet overwhelmingly common and thus safe society, membership in which was signalled by being in favor of Nixon.

Identity through belief, and loyalty to a group through acceptance of a doctrine, are hardly recent patterns of human behavior. Impressionism is a shared sensibility of sight and thought among men and women, as well as a style of painting. The Vienna Circle was a sort of club as well as a way of thinking. Heresies were movements as well as notions. But the members had names, they knew one another, they discussed and fought and disagreed among themselves about facts and ideas. Michael Harrington has said that the Bohemians of his generation might have been phonies just as the counterculturalists of the sixties might have been phonies. But if both can be accused of insincerity and intellectual exhibitionism, Harrington feels that there is a vital difference: his group was phony about first-class things: "Proust, Joyce, Kafka; Marx and Lenin; Beethoven and Balanchine." The counterculturalists were phony about second-class things: media-hyped music of the moment. They were as illiterate and ignorant as the bourgeois the Bohemians had abandoned.

Without taking up Harrington's judgments about what is first class, we can follow his lead in making a sharp distinction between the idea-groups of the past and the idea-groups of the present. In the present, the product-packaged media-distributed issue has inserted itself into the process of the exchange of ideas as a social function. In the present, the groups are ill-defined vague movements of mass sensibility toward mass-produced objects. The opinions that define the distinctions between ideas and people—the controversial issues the media talk so much about—are *primarily* serving a social function to the detriment of the knowledge function. More and more individuals play their conversation for the ghostlike audience of the "public" even when they are alone, because the ever present model of discourse and conversation is the manufactured and staged conversation of the media. The cliché, the stock response, the self-regarding attitude of the *salon,* where wit and bigotry hissed beneath the tinkling chandeliers of Tolstoy's St. Petersburg, have been democratized by the media and amplified to the ends of the earth.

As a result, whenever a person opens his mouth, in private as well as in public, his auditors are ready to purr or pounce at the code phrases they identify with certain vague groups they have learned to stereotype through the media. "Law and order" —he must be a racist. "Poverty breeds crime"—she must be a Northern liberal. "Defense of our land"—he must be a member of the military-industrial complex. The speaker then begins to become sensitive to these codes and so hedges his message that any originality is lost. Indeed, what might have been a presentation of thoughts that would have gladdened the heart of John Stuart Mill becomes a dreadful exercise in rote recital that would please any officer of the Thought Reform Schools of China.

Public debate and private discussion thus become contests of sensitivity to possible adverse reactions. It is no wonder that when definite goals are sought by definite groups they do not waste any time displaying their sensitivity. They demonstrate, they detonate, they demand, they actively non-negotiate. Reasonable discourse, as the surrealistic record of UN debates makes maddeningly clear, is no vehicle for democratic or any other kind of action. It is simply no longer available—so recourse is had to pressure which, in the extreme, is terrorism.

Terrorism and the strange autistic single-mindedness of the terrorist bring us, by a route never envisioned in Smith-Bruner-White or Lasswell, to the third function of opinion among individuals and of communication in society.

Externalization, the third function opinions perform for individuals, according to Smith-Bruner-White, is almost entirely a psychoanalytic as well as psychological notion. All internal conflicts are derived from our experiences, some of which may go back to early childhood. These inner conflicts often color views of the world outside and the struggles that rage in the outer, real world. Often enough, therefore, an opinion about politics or religion or even fashion may actually be a feeling about some internal conflict which can be allegorized in the external world and thus transferred to the external world. This assumption was behind the late Theodor W. Adorno's *Authoritarian Personality* studies: people were fascists because of their own internal drives and problems. Milton Rokeach expanded this view to include all sorts of political views of the far left as well as the far right—inner-motivated opinions were marked by rigidity and dogmatism for Rokeach and were more instructive about the mental make-up of the opinion holder than about the object of his opinion. This assumption was shared by Kenneth Kenniston in the sixties in his studies of alienated youth and campus radicals: much of their vehemence against college and national administrations was meant for their parents.

With some altering of detail, the following case from psychiatrist Karl Stern's *The Third Revolution* has been adapted to illustrate this function more vividly. There was an aging seaman who was retired and sought to live in Canada. He had been born in Norway and had spent his youth in both Canada and Norway and most of his subsequent life on the high seas. He was informed by the Canadian authorities that he did not have Canadian citizenship and would have to leave Canada. The information absolutely crushed the old sailor, who went into a deep depression. Such news would be hard for anyone to take; but the reaction of the sailor was extreme. Stern ascertained that the sailor's mother had been Canadian and his father had been Norwegian. His parents had divorced and lived in their countries of origin. As a child and adolescent, the old sailor had sailed between two countries, fatherland and motherland, fully accepted by neither. His avocation made him a man without a country. Retirement meant final landfall. He chose his mother but was rejected.

The story and the man moved the authorities to change their ruling. An official older than the sailor was chosen to tell him he could stay. His depression vanished.

Although Stern's case is more a reaction to an external event than an actively espoused opinion about external affairs, it most aptly points up the allegorization that events of the world provide for feelings within. When an opinion is put forward with unusual animus, the issue discussed is merely the top of the iceberg. The debates and arguments about McCarthyism in the fifties and about Vietnam in the sixties often were occasions for venting deep feelings about authority, loyalty, betrayal, faith, and exploitation on personal, non-political levels.

There is a point when this sort of influence on opinion becomes pathological and overwhelms the knowledge function and the social adjustment function. For normal individuals the three functions are in descending order of importance. For most opinions of importance for most people most of the time, externalization should be of minimal significance.

The totalistic obsession of the terrorist with his cause argues that the externalization function has taken over his faculties. The growing prevalence of terrorism increasingly argues that the quality of public discourse is being reduced even further away from the level of knowledge to the level of personal emotive release. Violent demonstration, refusal to let others speak, destruction of property as "symbolic utterance" are all events on the same road from reason and shared sensibility to autistic preoccupations paraded as social concern.

Lasswell's final function of social communication is the transmission of values and heritage from one generation to the next within a culture. The normal channels for this transmission have been the home, the school, the church. All three institutions have eroded from within as they have been besieged by the tumultuous technological, political, and economic upheavals of the century. Even the most conservative are preoccupied with defending institutions from further decay, with little time for using them as channels for values to the young. A teacher who must spend most of his precious time with students presenting his credentials is deprived of authority.

Just as the media have become the principal channels through which different groups communicate to one another in America, the media have replaced the schools, churches, and homes as sources for models of behavior, ideals to be followed, causes to espouse. Unfortunately, as in the social interchange function and the knowledge function, media use means media methods, and these methods are inexorably tied up with marketing and thus with propaganda.

The format and philosophical assumptions of the television commercial become the model for channeling values. Videotapes, audiotapes, textbook formats, records, slides—the multimedia approach, the manufactured product as a solution to ignorance and lack of discipline—have long become entrenched in the school system, with educators apologetic about the dullness of the lecture method, lacking as it is in production values and what amounts to audience participation (not student performance).

Aggressive evangelists and established churches are engrossed in method and media usage. Some fundamentalist groups, untrammeled by the self-doubt that afflicts the more traditional churches, have large institutions with very sophisticated equipment and advanced technical training in the use of multimedia presentations.

We have not yet reached the stage when Dad and Mom will have pre-recorded color videotape presentations for their children on such topics as Cleaning Your Room: The Fun and the Challenge. But of course the thousands of situation comedies dealing with family life, the "Modern Living" sections of the newsmagazines, *Reader's Digest* homilies and reprints, how-to paperbacks—these are virtually doing the same thing at less

cost. If there should be a specialized market out there somewhere, there is no doubt that a firm can develop personalized
multimedia parental presentations for "that specially privileged
child" to make for more effective family communications. In
Odyssey 2001, Kubrick has captured the extreme paradigm of
this trend in the vast Hilton carousel in the sky where people
deal with machines easily but are uncomfortable face-to-face.

In this universe of discourse, with packaging and format
specialists in charge, with one-way communication by machine,
personal opinions are of less and less utility for knowledge or
for social adjustment. Increasingly, they are a help in external-
izing conflicts and problems—but not in resolving them. The
result is a sort of perverse synergy—a multitude of causes reinforcing one another in pushing reasoned debate out of court and
in facilitating and encouraging propaganda barrages of slogans
on a mass of disengaged, lost souls who are ready to agree if it
means acceptance in some ghostlike group whose image has
been publicized, ready to oppose if it releases some pent-up
hostilities of private origin.

One hundred years and more after John Stuart Mill, freedom
of expression is become a thriving business, but the language
that is used and the causes that are served would be unrecogniz-
able to the rational individualist of the nineteenth century. The
ideal forum of debate which he sought in his own time is farther
than ever from realization. The forces preventing it in America
are not like the crude and harsh repression of Moscow and
Peking. Here, instead, there is the bland manufacture of all
opinion according to marketing formulae. There is the reduction, above all, of individual voices to typecast roles according
to marketing needs. There is the blending of public issues and
government into popular culture and entertainment and the
application of entertainment standards (i.e., those which are
attention-holding at the level of the lowest common denominator) to public utterance. These forces have transformed the
forum in which ideas are presented and heard.

part two
THE BUREAUCRACY OF ENTERTAINMENT

eight
Entertaining Ideas

Agnes Nixon feels that she has a public-service obligation to deal with issues. Norman Lear is proud of the controversial issues that he has dealt with. Both Mrs. Nixon and Mr. Lear are creators and controllers of very large and successful business enterprises, supplying television with season after season of predictable product, manufactured uniformly with impressive quality control. Mrs. Nixon supervises the writing of a number of long-term daytime soap operas that are distributed nationally and widely by both syndicates and networks. Mr. Lear supervises a number of evening programs that are commonly referred to as situation comedies.

Soap operas and situation comedies, of such central programming importance to the most mass and influential of the media, have achieved an importance and authority characteristic of all media celebrity. Fiction and reality are strangely, yet inevitably, intermingled in the Mediaworld of which they constitute such a large part.

Both formats of television entertainment have created a vast body of satellite media fare in print. There are magazines which tell the same story that is being unfolded on the screen of the soap opera, for those who may have let the demands of their nonmedia life interfere with their viewing schedule. There are magazines that give extra-plot details about the actors and actresses who play in both formats. The actors' and actresses' lives off screen have, it is felt, an effect on their performances and at times, in the case of serious illness or major life decisions, a necessary impact on the plots they have plodded through over the years. They must be written out or up to conform to "real" needs. For literally millions of fans—and that is the appropriate word—the thoughts and actions and conflicts of these celebrity-actor-characters have taken on a special meaning that they cannot find in flesh-and-blood unscripted immediate acquaintances nor in their own lives or thoughts, except as observers.

The millions of viewers of these programs and the heavy investment of time and interest beyond the mere time of the actual broadcasts on the part of devotees have made of the principal characters and the actors that portray these characters international celebrities. Due to the universal media practice of paid endorsements, the public expects celebrities to say things about products with authority. Due to the use of celebrities in charity fund-raising and political campaigns, the public expects celebrities to have views about controversial public issues. The expectation of pronouncements springing from the mouths of celebrities has changed the very idea of celebrity and charged it with the added meaning of authority. The aura of celebrity surrounding staple soap-opera characters gives added weight to what they have to say—as actors paid to endorse products, presidential candidates, or cancer research—and even in the *persona* of the character they have portrayed for so long to so many that their identity in the public forum is that of the character. Actors long identified with sober and super-honest law enforcement roles, for instance, make ideal endorsers of insurance, banks, and credit card memberships.

It is a small step from the actor as celebrity-authority to the character in the soap opera or situation comedy as celebrity-authority within the frame of the script. The views and opinions of soap-opera characters have become influential, just as their hair styles, automobile preference, and mannerisms have become influential.

With such enormous influence, it is no wonder that writer-executives like Mrs. Nixon and Mr. Lear feel such concern about the subject matter of their programs. Caught up in the media agenda of packaged issues, the assigned topics of discussion and interest for the moment, mass media drama writers want to be with the trends. As issues provide pre-sell interest in periodicals and broadcast news, they also provide maintenance of interest in long-term program series. And the series treatment of the issue can keep the issue itself alive a little longer for use by non-fiction writers, documentary film makers, news commentators, and assignment editors of major media. To complete the circle, the celebrity-characters of the series become more realistic, more celebrated, and more authoritative for the audience, the more they are obediently concerned with current issues.

What will the writers have the characters do and say relative to the issues and controversies of the day? As politicians depend on votes, programs depend on ratings. Therefore, nothing will be said or done by any character to offend any appreciable group in the paying audience. If the character is considered evil or a buffoon, then he or she may well mouth some lines that are calculated to be out of tune with prevailing newsmagazine or television commentary.

In the late sixties the plot of an Alfred Hitchcock film called for the heroine to go to bed with the hero without benefit of matrimonial documents. There was strenuous and outraged objection on the part of the public. Since fornication, adultery, lesbianism, even child molestation had already been part of not a few films by that time, the outcry was due not to objections to the plot, but rather to the casting. The heroine was actress Julie Andrews, who had been cast in bland musicals, usually attended by squads of adoring children (not her own). Her roles in the past dominated the public expectation of her future roles.

No doubt Miss Andrews, like Sean Connery/James Bond, deliberately sought to break this artistically crippling typecasting. Such a departure may have been good for their careers as artists, but introducing variety and range is also permitting unpredictability. It is bad business.

Therefore the popular culture drama of television and of mass films have characters and roles that mirror and intensify the sensitivity of centrist politicians and newsmen-celebrities to what might give offense. Most careful self-censorship is exercised by these men lest anyone react to a code-cliché and type them as racists, or communists, or elitists, or militants—or any of the many things one could be other than mainstream and acceptable. Within the framework of the soap opera or situation comedy, the sympathetic characters will show the same sensitivity, and for the same reason. Popular support reflected in the ratings keeps shows on the air as votes keep politicians in office.

Successfully managed demand requires reliable forecasting of repeated sales of the same product. To achieve this, each successive edition, as it were, of the product must closely imitate its predecessor. For mass-marketed hamburgers and apples, the inner taste must be as predictable as the outer form. There can be no surprises after the purchase or the purchase will not be repeated. After viewers settle down for one more visit to Dodge City, or the command deck of the starship *Enterprise* or "The Little House on the Prairie," they know exactly what to expect from the continuing cast. Such affectionate anticipation of an accustomed, yet paradoxically exotic, atmosphere and situation, peopled with old friends, springs from the same sources as the comforting excitement felt by regular visitors to Baker Street. But market dependence on ratings and inspiration by committee reduce reliability to rigid repetition. The patterns of Conan Doyle or Dickens are predictably familiar, but they allowed for intrinsically motivated variations. Weekly or monthly editions of mass-produced TV series draw their very variety from a bin of familiar gimmicks, much like the accessories that "customize" Detroit cars.

Rigid formats render any more than minimal variation bizarre or zany. Consequently, parody is the most successful form of media humor, at its best on television, the most mass and thus most rigid medium. The favored form of army and prison humor, parody is the sublimated revenge of the regimented.

As part of the same marketing system that has so successfully packaged ideas and events as "issues," popular culture, with its necessarily routine predictability, is notoriously inhospitable to art. Reality is incorrigibly plural because it is a collectivity of irreducible particulars—often unmanageably so. Thus everyone has daily recourse to the cliché and the stereotype. Art keeps this daily recourse from becoming an exclusive method of dealing with the world. Turner forces us to see particular skies; Tolstoy compels acquaintance with an unrepeatable Anna. In short, archetypes are not stereotypes and the universal is not commonplace.

Russell Nye, who has devoted exquisite patience to pounds of popular culture from forgotten decades, notes that dependence on the technology of duplication requires that the content of the piece of popular culture be essentially a verification of the familiar. The characterization is accurate—it is the soul of the star system, after all, to bring back the familiar in a slightly novel package to guaranteed customers. But it could be misunderstood, in that verification might mean the application of some kind of genuinely artistic insight that transforms the commonplace dross of everyday unreflective experience to the gold of universal and timeless significance. Nye does not necessarily mean this. Closer to his meaning is the use of the same word by Walker Percy in his novel, *The Moviegoer.* For Percy, addictive moviegoers find the world of film bigger than the world of their own drab, humdrum existence. They would have no trouble answering Dick Cavett's rhetorical question: "Which is more real, the screen or life?" Thus, when a movie used a location that a moviegoer had experienced in his real, everyday life, that location was "verified." It was given significance by being subsumed into the more real world, the scripted, simplified, mood-musiced "movieworld."

Mass-distributed popular culture is a verification of the familiar, because the familiar sells. But the familiar in question is not that which is directly experienced—it is the familiar stereotype of previous artifacts of mass culture. It is a closed world, divorced from the real world of common and even uncommon experience. It is a predictable world of its own—seen by those who sell it as valuable precisely for this quality of escape into the familiar forms of mass culture itself. The self-contained world of predictable and familiar stereotypes is most clearly seen in the comic strip, many of which are not at all comic but rather melodramatic.

The characters are changeless. Little Orphan Annie, Dick Tracy, Brenda Starr, Batman and Robin, Charlie Brown—they have not aged nor adjusted to new times. Their very appearance incarnates the literal meaning of stereotype. The presuppositions they have about the real world remain the same over decades, with occasional obligatory episodes dealing with "issues," such as women's liberation, according to their fixed mode of conduct. Of all Americans, real or imagined, comic strip caricatures are the most sure to observe traditional holidays, from Thanksgiving to St. Valentine's Day.

This, of course, is their appeal. Daily or weekly one can ritually bathe in this world of childhood simplicity and share little jokes in the office by transposing the comic clichés to local situations. Along with the bulk of sportscasting and sports writing, the comic strip is one of the most reliably constant aspects of our times. Before the advent of parody-prone TV serials, the comics were alone in providing, as they still provide, *The National Lampoon, Mad,* and so-called Underground Strips with a rich menagerie of pre-programmed marionettes for bizarre parody and soft pornography. The success of the parody is based on the same foundation as the success of the original: utterly predictable behavior by utterly predictable figures. It is this familiar that is verified, not the familiar of experience.

Thus a new comic strip, a new TV series, a new film made for block-and-blitz booking, a new novel designed for maximum sales—all must follow the formula of demand management and mass marketing. There is no difference in principle between the concocting of a new TV series and the designing of a new cosmetic appearance for an automobile, a new packaging for a cigarette, or a new type of convenience food. The concocter, or producer, banks on the predictability of the public, even as the public is counting on the predictability of his product. It is a hall of mirrors.

It is a tribute to the persistence of human creativity that occasionally, however rarely, the system partially accommodates an artist who also is very strong and demanding of his managers in the interests of his work. It is a tribute to the endurance of the human desire for excellence and integrity that some managers and financiers, despite enormous pressures, have accepted risk because of belief in an artist or an idea. Once a great artist has broken through the demands of the system for predictability of format to reach the higher form of predictability—the expectation of quality—it takes no courage or intelligence to back him.

The mass marketplace becomes a focus, therefore, of a variety of conservatisms: the proverbial conservatism of business meets the natural reluctance to accept new art, new technique, new visions. The technology of duplication adds one more conservative influence on popular culture: that of the scientific and engineering communities, which have stoned their prophets with as much reliability as Church and Academy. The technology of distribution to a faceless horde, ever growing since the development of mass literacy and of media that do not require literacy, places on all popular culture the final back-breaking determinism toward the routine and hackneyed: the necessity of the middleman.

If individuals innovate, while groups resist, middlemen are the marshals of the conservatisms of groups. Middlemen, needed for money and contracts and access to distribution systems, necessarily insert themselves between the artist and the public, as they do between the farmer and the consumer. The artist cannot write to please himself. He cannot write to please his public. He must make something that will meet the expectations of the middleman about what will please the public—that is, sufficiently large numbers of the public. At times this brings about an alienation of the artist from his audience that parallels the alienation of the worker from his job. The middleman, be he agent, executive producer, programming vice-president, publisher, or managing editor, may despise the very artifact he is promoting as beneath his attention except as a money-making instrument of marketing. The artist may despise his own work, but believe it necessary in order to become known and thus have a chance to create independently. At times perhaps even a majority of individuals who pay for a book, film, or show may actually detest what they pay for, but feel compelled to experience what promotion has decreed popular. In short, it is likely that popular culture successes are essentially verifications of what influential middlemen expect the public to buy, based on what it has paid for before. Thus the ability to predict the popular, which may be allied with an ability to manage demand, has become the most prized talent in the world of popular culture; it is more in demand than the skill of artist or writer.

A. E. Housman once said that he recognized great poetry by the peculiar tingling sensation he felt at the back of his neck whenever he read or heard the lines. Greatness for Housman was a degree of excellence appreciated by critics and readers over a period of time. He was not predicting "hit" poems. Lew Grade of Associated Television has had a remarkable career as a predicter of the financial success of as yet unproduced films or TV series from the scripts or one-page "concepts" he reads. In the marketing frame of reference, Lord Grade's feelings are far more significant than Housman's tinglings. It is doubtful whether any lyricist would have read his lines to Housman in the hope of making the poet's hair stand on end.

The judgment of the middleman is thus necessarily far more conservative than the judgment of a critic about art, or of a scientist about innovation—and the latter are already conservative by nature; they look to the past for touchstones and standards to measure new creation. The middleman, of course, is not consulting touchstones or standards. He is comparing sales figures and demographics of previous programs or books or films or records that most resemble the product he has been offered. He may be consulting his nose, his guts, his hunches. But the nose is sniffing the public, not the art.

The middleman's frame of reference is also far narrower. Unlike critics and scientists, he cannot be bothered with vast sweeps of historical development. Their touchstones and standards, whether relevant or not, are at least comprehensive and take the long view. The middleman is concerned with the most recent successful popular culture products. In fact, there is a money premium on fresh data supplied by market researchers. No respectable middleman is interested in last year's Nielson ratings when he can get today's.

Middlemen are always looking for *another,* not a new or original. They are looking for *another* of recent vintage. No agent or executive producer will cry "Another Hamlet!" with the tone of "Eureka!" If he has a very developed historical sense, he may shout joyfully, "Another *Gone with the Wind!*" This is not to say that the middleman is some kind of insensitive yahoo—any given middleman may have far more artistic sensitivity than the average academic hack or high-culture Puritan. It is to say that such sensitivity should not be taken to the office.

As middlemen look to the market for their cues of what to

buy and promote, professional writers and artists look to the practical necessities of the medium of their choice as a guide for their invention of event, circumstance, character and plot. Some of these inventions are brilliantly executed, if not intrinsically motivated. The Transporter Room of the starship *Enterprise* of "Star Trek," for instance, was a necessary plot device to get variety of circumstance in and out of an essentially claustrophobic set, without the time- (and money-) consuming devices of landing craft, of having the huge ship itself land and take off, or of other portrayals of movement. The Transporter is instantaneous, uses brilliant special effects, and contributes to the aura of the fantastic, while it solves a practical problem imposed by the formula of a TV series.

Writers for series are all given guidelines to keep them in tone and within budget on any given show. A working knowledge of how programs are filmed or taped is of invaluable aid to a writer. Inexorably, this means that much of what happens is dictated by the formula of the market rather than the inner inevitabilities of the writer's invention.

Action-adventure, by far the most popular genre on television for the past twenty years, portrays conflict cheaply and efficiently by staging physical fights. Sixty- to ninety-minute programs, the favored length of a prime-time action-adventure, inevitably resolve the tensions that have been created in the first three quarters, at times very cleverly, by rapid and intrinsically incredible acts of violence or panic, improbable confessions, unspeakably fortunate strokes of luck. Master craftsmen can frequently arrange all of this with some wit and style, but the point is that they are writing for a formula, not for themselves or for an audience.

Since less money and less technology are involved, there may be less restrictive pressure on writers for popular print media, but they too write for a formula made to fit a magazine designed for a market.

It would be vain and repetitious to hurl imprecations at the vulgarity and tinsel and superficiality of mass culture and its inhospitality to art and originality. It would also be to miss the point about mass culture. The machinery of mass culture, after all, has marketed this book. Publishing is part of the mass culture machine and far more people have read far more books of "high culture" in so-called mass society than in any previous society. Within the vastness of parallel mass distribution systems, there is still room for the patron of excellence to read books, hear recordings and see films of breathtaking artistry.

Nonetheless, popular culture, in the sense of market-managed formula-productions for page, stage, and screen, is the overwhelming captor of the public's willing attention. Art has been engulfed by entertainment and entertainment has been thoroughly bureaucratized, as the modern state has been bureaucratized (and as the world of work and sport have been systematized), according to formulae and formats.

It is understandable, but wrong-headed, to sneer at popular culture artifacts as poor art by failed artists who have sold out. The case is rather that the comic strip has moved up to more sophisticated forms and by sheer volume has distracted us from attending to the real art that is still around us. Entertainment has become mechanized and ubiquitous—and identified with what is revealingly termed "production values." The big-business necessity of demand management and the mass-production possibilities of new kinds of technologies of duplication have therefore conspired to make of entertainment and information creatures of bureaucracy.

Bureaucracy specializes in the management of life according to fixed formulae for the disparate fragments into which it requires human existence to be parceled. Bureaucracy confers legitimacy, status, and order on institutions and individuals. The attendant ills that bureaucracy inevitably generates—sterility, boredom, alienation, loss of vital purpose, formalism—are well known, universally experienced, and copiously commented upon. These very same defects are often cited as marks of mass media output—lack of imagination, tedious formulae, lack of creativity, loss of contact with the audience—without the realization that they are the side effects, not the purpose, of the news and entertainment bureaucracies. Like any bureaucracy, their main goal is to endure and grow under stable conditions.

nine
The Media Community

As we have seen, there is a great pressure from above—from the managers and owners and makers of the media—for predictability. There is also a complementary great pressure from below—from paying customers, the viewers, listeners, and readers—for the familiar: not the familiar of life, but the familiar of mass culture formats. Market demand for the familiar is managed well, but it is not created from nothing but the wishes of entrepreneurs. It has spontaneous origins in the nature of modernized life.

The clarity and order of the long bourgeois summer, which gave definition to bohemianism itself, is over. Customs and manners, the well-drilled rules of public behavior, are too feeble now to ease our meetings and dealings and disputes with expected ritual. Unlike hierarchies of wolves and chickens, modern Americans peck without order, which may account for the explosive expansion of litigation among professional associates and friends.

What has been called folk culture, the distinctive rites and rules and arts of an ethnic group, provided an almost instinctive set of norms within which individuals found a place to act and feel. Elites, by definition set above the necessities of parochial groups, could also look to world literature and art for touchstones of right behavior and cultivated sensibility. Although obviously Russian, or English, or Irish, or French, or Japanese, or Kenyan, or Argentine in provenance, literature and art are essentially interfolk and international in that they deal with the consciousness of an individual as he or she meets basic human experiences of grief, growth, triumph, failure, love, and death.

What folk or fairy tales do for children, literature and art do for more cosmopolitan adults: locate their experiences and feelings within cultural history and give them community meaning. Covering millennia of time and continents of geography, literature and art nonetheless legitimate private feelings.

On different levels folk and high culture provide the same thing. They partially heal the wound of individuality by uniting one's inner feelings and private joys and sorrows to that of a community—either the immediate community of ethnic peers or the more sophisticated and less easily apprehended community of man himself. Folk culture does this not only through its art and stories, through festivals and rituals for special occasions, but also through the humble customs and ordinary costumes of everyday life. High culture addresses itself more immediately to the inner sensibility of the more sophisticated (and therefore perhaps somewhat alienated) adult, whose sense of self is both more particular and more expansive than that of those defined totally by ethnic identity.

Although, as Dwight Macdonald has pointed out, folk culture is anonymously produced over long periods of time by the genius of a people whereas high culture is the distinctive work of an individual genius, nevertheless, both types are profoundly impregnated with the heaviness of time and tradition. The folk are such because of their deeds and sufferings through time; the great artist is part or founder of a school, which is understood as a development from, or a rejection of, a previous school. Bestowing senses of community on its receivers, high and folk cultures are also examples of community in themselves.

The primary criticism of the quality of popular culture has

been fundamentally on aesthetic grounds; on comparison, a given example of popular mass culture is shown as shallow, or factitious, or formulaic in the light of so-called high culture standards. The primary defense of the quality of popular mass culture has been in terms of politics—on analysis, a given example of popular mass culture is shown to be (not surprisingly) precisely what a large number of people are willing to pay for. To look down on what a large number of people apparently enjoy is snobbish and out of place in a democratic nation. Generally speaking, artists and writers deplore most facets of mass culture that deal with entertainment or the distribution of art. Generally speaking, social scientists praise the democratic features and elevating potential of mass distribution systems for popular art. The artists look at the work; the social scientists look at the consuming groups. They tend to disagree, or seem to disagree, because they simply are not talking about the same thing.

It will be instructive to look at the mass media, particularly the most characteristic mass medium, television, not from the viewpoint of aesthetic dogmatism nor from the mountain of democratic theology, but merely from the viewpoint of cultural function. In verifying the familiar the media have generated a type of surrogate stability once provided by local communities and have presented a kind of standard for feelings once provided by literature. Oxymoronic as it may sound, Mediaworld is mass community and instant tradition.

Television news programming is the epitome of media as community. The central figure of television news programming is the anchor. A word derived from sports and business, the "anchor" or "anchorman" was the last runner of a relay team, the man who tied the whole team effort together and gave it meaning by his final and crucial performance. Involved business arrangements require an anchor as an integrating personality and frequently as a symbol of integrity and fair dealing. Presently, the first meaning that comes to mind is of the television anchorman (or, more recently, anchorperson) who ties together the disparate and chaotic segments of news film from all over the world or from all over the city. His presence also lends a note of integrity and truthfulness to the proceedings.

Because of his or her importance, the selection of an anchorperson is one of the most vital decisions ever made by broadcast management. News broadcasts are most closely identified with management in the public mind and they are presented and labeled by management to enhance this identification. The anchorperson is the personification of the abstract corporation which owns the network or local station on which he appears. In 1976 the moving of anchorperson Barbara Walters from NBC to ABC created sensational interest and coverage and her very large salary symbolized her importance to the corporation.

One of the top three broadcast news consultants of America advises management to look for one quality in a prospective anchorperson. Although difficult to put into words, that quality can be understood by analogy, says the consultant. If someone dies in the family, who among all the brothers and sisters and uncles and aunts is chosen to break the news "to dear old Mom"? The quality that makes one instinctively chosen as the vessel for bearing grief to a loved one is the quality broadcast management must look for in their candidates. Television, the consultant reminds them, is an intimate medium; it is in people's homes, frequently their bedrooms. The news of the world is harsh and cruel; it should be broken by a trusted confidant. The cognate concepts "familiar" and "family" are closely related to all media functions.

To further insure the continuity and familiarity that an anchorperson provides, some formats provide two equal co-anchors. Many stations and one network have man-woman co-anchors. When co-anchors are used, the loss of one through illness, dispute, or merely vacation, does not interfere with the personal relationship that has been built up with an audience, as the loss of one anchorperson would. When this format is combined with the use of a presenting "news team" in the studio, the family-familiar atmosphere is considerably strengthened. News teams come in two styles: the crisp service personnel, dressed in airline collegiate, and the hard-working journalists, straight from steaming typewriters. The former appear on stylized sets that borrow much from the space program; the latter perform in the "newsroom," the workroom, that borrows much from *The Front Page*. With the relatively recent appearance of young women on the sets, and their increasing number, contemporary television news formats more and more resemble the family settings so long favored by television melodrama and comedy.

As the family function of the news teams increase, the news functions decrease. Viewers can go on a diet with the local TV weatherman, quit smoking with the sportscaster, learn of bargains and supermarket swindles from their local lady journalist. Television non-news is broad and varied: gossip columnists, financial advice, medical reassurance and ample stimulation for hypochondria, Miss Lonelyhearts, crusading lawyers protecting the little people. In short, television news and radio stations with the "all news all the time" format have done nothing more than imitate their print predecessors, for the same reasons but with more intense, and perhaps not intended, results.

There are sound business reasons for the proliferation of non-news, which inevitably takes the form of service information and "human interest" stories. Compared to alternate formats of equal cost, local news is easily the most saleable programming to advertisers, because the messages they buy are surrounded with an atmosphere of importance, credibility, and friendly advice. Old movies, game shows, and cartoons, the cheap alternates that local stations feel they can afford, cannot provide this. There is simply not enough news, in the precise sense, each day, let alone each hour, to fill out all the time or all the pages necessary to carry all the advertising that can be sold.

The result of these formats in broadcasting and print is to create audiences who see themselves as members of an extended community, "loyal" listeners/viewers/readers of their "own" station or newspaper or news team. This is by design, of course; it is the essence of mass marketing through demand management. But it also has the effect of creating a very special kind of consumer community—only metaphorically akin to the bogus fellowship of the Pepsi(-Cola) Generation. Television, particularly, presents all these "community" services through the star personalities of anchorpersons and members of the news team, at once celebrities and intimate confidants.

With competing media each offering such services, most often in the media language of the television commercial, which offers salvation through product or purchase, the overall consequence is that virtually all of the psychological and physical needs once thought provided by tribe, village, town, or neighborhood face-to-face contacts with familiar friends and fixed figures have now been supplied, on a mass-produced scale, by the media. The modern wound of alienation from a permanent membership in a proud tribe, with its supportive folk culture and folkways, has been soothed by the analgesic aerosol of mass culture and media role models.

Decades ago, studies indicated that daytime radio soap operas provided two essential services for the housewives who worked alone in their apartments or then-new suburban homes. The programs gave them a sense of companionship and provided models of problem-solving they felt applicable to their own lives. The medium was a more antiseptic service than the overcrowded and non-private old neighborhoods ever could offer over the back fence or across the airshaft. Subsequent mobility and suburban sprawl have placed more and more Americans, male and female, in the isolated position of the housewife (already a quaint job description) of yesteryear. In the media community, we are all housewives getting companionship and friendly advice from slick professionals we can see as well as hear on a far greater scale and over a much broader range. Human life has been compartmentalized into varied sets of technical problems soluble, in theory, by the appropriately prepared technician. Even death requires a thanatologist.

Soap operas and situation comedies, special reports and daily features, self-help best sellers in cooking, in sex, in "peace of mind" provide a continual fountain of reassurance, comfort, and practical tips. Media formats require that living be fragmented into specialties, just as bureaucracy has divided procedures into separate jurisdictions, with separate and special forms. Such machine-mediated bureaucratic advice and aid, while designed to be marketed precisely to meet the needs of the lonely and alienated consuming audience, in a way exacerbates the condition it feeds on. The hungry sheep look up and are fed canned tape.

The popularity of live concerts and appearances, the very use of the term, "live," underlines the fundamental dissatisfaction felt by all groups for the remote and unresponding taped image. A variety of technical strategies have been devised to overcome this feeling. Taping before live audiences, rather than adding a laugh-and-applause track to a completed tape (a practice still in use after twenty years), gives the later audiences at home the illusion of participation and simultaneity, both of which substitute for the sense of occasion evoked by live performance.

Live rock concerts, with their raw emotion, lack of professional polish, orgiastic audience participation—the very qualities which repel older Americans—are not so much adolescent and young adult manifestations of indifference to talent as they are a rebellion against the antiseptic, depersonalized, pretested mass popular culture that formed the bulk of the so-called television generation's contact with entertainment and art. The passing but intense popularity of "Monty Python," from England, and "Saturday Night," from New York, among young adults and teenagers was due to the same causes. They were zany and bizarre, rich in parody. They did not mock the world so much as the media community. They were unpolished and self-indulgent, without discipline or editing. Yet again, these very characteristics which repel older Americans trained to respect competence (from Astaire to Nureyev) win over the television generation, who frequently equate polish with phony pre-packaged formats from the bureaucracy of entertainment. Lack of preparation, formerly an insult to paying customers, is now seen as a gesture of sincerity and friendship to an alienated crowd fed up with key-punched cards. This "wild" style is currently being packaged for increasing videotape airing on late-night schedules.

A further irony is that the record industry, the basic promoter of live concerts and all the grades of rock from acid to z, is one of the most heavily capitalized, conglomerated, vertically integrated industries in business. Heavily dependent on high technology and gifted engineers who can create sounds that could never come from a human throat or hand instrument, every rock group of importance requires expensive equipment and expensive lawyers. Thus, even the popular culture billed as "revolutionary" and pumped through the media system is both technical and bureaucratic from source to audience.

The mass media market system has taken over the amateur, as it were, functions of the folk communities (gossip, advice, practical wisdom, music, festivals) as well as the creeds and codes behind these customs, and has professionally packaged them, following the mechanical model of the antiseptic television commercial—the unitary exemplar of media language.

In the frenetically mobile nation of perpetual migrants the media make up the common calendar. National festivals from July Fourth to Thanksgiving are media events promoted into occasions for hypermercantilism. Media events, in turn, from the Superbowl to the autumnal rite of the New Season of New Programming, are national festivals. The weekly list of events is *TV Guide.* Common conversation is the *news:* a list of topics formed in about equal measure by uncontrollable events and the Associated Press Day Book (a list of events planned for media coverage each day). Mutual acquaintances are that fluid troop of celebrities who move in and out of the pages of *People* and on and off the sets of "Today" or "Tonight," whose very titles reveal their true function. Finally, community concerns are *issues,* as we have seen, the running themes that assignment editors, politicians, and promoters manage for the sake of ordering and continuing their output, in the best bureaucratic tradition.

The code of the folk community was based on a creed. The creed may have been explicitly formulated or may not have been, but it was embodied in the heroes and heroines of legends, tales and stories. The media community, of course, has a creed implicit in the assumptions of instrumentalism that govern the transitional forum for public opinion. These assumptions leak out in the roles written for stars in the scripts of television series and soap operas, reinforcing the slogan awareness of the public to market-required issues. For many, the characters of popular culture narratives have replaced the heroes and heroines of folk culture, on the one hand, and the archetypal figures of literature, on the other.

As a business that cannot offend customers, the mass media exist in a market that overlays a collection of ethnic and occupational groups that have paid advocates and agents to represent their interests and, above all, their image, in the media community. These groups are the ones that cannot be offended. Thus the role models, as they are tentatively called today, provided by the media tend to be bland and inoffensive—suppressed and repressed characters or fearless and irresistible forces for good in a world of stark evil/good contrasts.

This creed, instrumentalism blunted by the fear of giving offense, has been explicitly translated into a code of behavior for the images on our screens and tubes which are increasingly seen as the types that will provide us with models to imitate.

The Motion Picture Production Code, as the later Television

Code, is fundamentally a marketing, not a moral, necessity. Films can recoup considerable production investments and go on to show a profit only if they are shown to very large audiences, which must be gathered from very wide geographic areas. Any film that requires special editing for each area of the market into which it is distributed contradicts the fundamental law of successful mass marketing: ever-increasing returns on fixed-cost units. As with the marketing of apples and autos, the lowest common denominator is sought. In this context, the LCD is negative; no scenes or dialogue are distributed to mass audiences that might offend anyone enough to cause legislative or judicial censorship or provoke punitive boycotts.

In the early twenties, Hollywood agents made a number of field trips to the vast heartland of the American market between the coasts. By direct inquiry and observation they drew up a list of elements in films that triggered objections that might prove costly to film makers. This catalogue of potential offenses was graded into two categories: the absolutely forbidden (to those who wanted to reach a large market) and the dangerous, which required careful treatment. The then Hays Office distributed this list to the film community, where it was adopted as a guide for safe production. (Established in 1922 and called for ten years after its director, former Postmaster General Will Hays, the Hays Office was the public relations arm of the Producers and Distributors Association—a precursor of Jack Valenti's Motion Picture Association.) The business wizards who founded the big studios knew that film, as a wordless medium, was the ideal product for distribution to a polyglot nation as it would later be, with sound-track dubbing, the international form of entertainment. Where language was overcome, cultural taboos could not be allowed to interfere.

The Production Code, developed under the aegis of the Hays Office and since amended a number of times to reflect changing market conditions, was the ultimate practical result of this commercial insight. Television distributors, the networks and

syndicates, the heirs to film as the most mass and most international of the media, have learned from the earlier generation of
film bureaucracies and have inherited their headaches as well
as their stratagems.

It was not until the thirties that an articulate code was actually written out, complete with a preamble and philosophic
jargon. The original grocery list of forbidden fruits came about
from fear of failure to sell film broadly enough to large markets.
The new and more codified, as it were, Code came about because of fear of a national boycott of films on the part of irate
citizens organized as the National Legion of Decency.

Although unquestionably spearheaded by the well-organized
Catholic Church, the Legion was truly an interfaith movement
in its origins, endorsed by *The New York Times* and constituted
by an amalgam of Protestant, Jewish, and civic organizations.
Economics was arguably the reason for the Legion's phenome-
nal success in the thirties. It was the bureaucratic form of the
Deuteronomic Law, one of the more reliable generalities about
collective human behavior. The thirties were the years of the
Depression and Hard Times. The Deuteronomic Law has three
parts: (1) we suffer because we are guilty; (2) we are guilty
because of what we have done; (3) we must punish whoever is
to blame for what we have done. At that time the depravities
of the cities of the plain, notably New York and Los Angeles,
were seen as reaching into virtuous America and corrupting the
previously innocent. The films were the instrument of this evil
influence and their filth and glorification of criminal violence
(the early thirties had James Cagney putting a lot of lead in a
lot of middle Americans) were corrupting society.

The new Code forbade basically two kinds of things: the
provocative presentation of sex and the sympathetic presentation of (violent) crime. Although the Code was mechanistically
conceived and applied (what was or was not provocative was
determined by lights, inches, and selected parts of the anatomy;
what was or was not sympathetic was determined by explicit

lines of dialogue—perhaps the origin of the voice-over at the end of a film detailing in rapid order the justice later meted out to the bad guys), it also had some ideologically determined proscriptions against certain subjects: drugs, communism, anti-patriotism. The fundamental presupposition of the Code was that film would influence behavior because it glorified and glamorized whatever it presented and whomever it presented (stars and issues). There was also the notion, perennial in all censorship efforts, that film was too widespread to be left unchecked. Sophisticated Broadway theatregoers did not need a Code, but farm boys and shop girls in dark halls did need guidance. The new literacy and cheap newsprint of the nineteenth century had sparked the same repressive fears about reading.

In the fifties, the Legion and the Code began to lose force. In the sixties, the Code was revised out of existence and replaced by a rating system. By the late sixties, a time of prosperity and cultural revolution, the Legion had gone away with the Deuteronomic Law. Television had replaced movies as the most mass of the media. The censorship pressure was eased on the latter, therefore, and transferred to the former. Further, good economics required that films assert their marginal differentiation from television, a competitor for media dollars. The rating system advertised most effectively what had been a selling point of the film industry for a long time: films are for adults; moviegoers do not have to put up with the kiddie fare of television. Necessity, once again, became a moral virtue.

Television, reaching millions of people every hour, inherited the early cycle of film code problems. The hard economic times of the early seventies revitalized the Deuteronomic Law. Television was routinely denounced as the source of national unrest and loss of American prestige abroad. New and powerful boycott and pressure groups cursed television for corrupting youth through the portrayal of sex, violence, and drugs. Some of the violence the networks have been denounced for was in the form of cartoons, recycled material from the film world, where it had been seen as harmless matinee material.

Television is now coming to the end of the same code cycle that film experienced. New technologies for new media—cable, videocasettes, laser discs—give promise of electronic distribution to selective audiences, targeted by computer, thus threatening the market advantage of broadcasting with more sophisticated multiple "narrowcasting." To compete with this as yet ghostlike rival, television is trying to differentiate and "narrowcast" in terms of time if not in terms of channels. As with the film-rating system, Family Viewing Time is the politically acceptable way of stating what is really at stake: non-Family Viewing Time, where TV will now be able to compete with R-rated films (to say nothing of showing R-rated films), pay TV, and cable services.

The circle nears completion. The codes, which were a practical way of avoiding legal and marketing troubles by anticipating objections from local and ethnic cultures, have now become a way of introducing previously objectionable material. Rating systems pay official tribute to folk objections by labeling material that has been proven successful at the box office or in market research as suitable for mature audiences or of possible offense to the sensitive. (The sensitive cannot, it would seem, be mature.) It is a systems version of the banned-in-Boston sales hype. As Milton said of a similar procedure centuries ago, "the punishing of wits enhances their authority."

There could not be a more apt instance of the bureaucratic substitute for community functions that the media systematically provide. Media fare does indeed contain models for life and for life-style—that is the presupposition of the codes and of the objections to the codes. The material codified and labeled is defined by its marketing destination, not by its intrinsic content. The labeling is done by assigned apparatchiks, separate from the producers and distributors, but paid by them. They are guided by prior lists of specific images and words which are mechanistically, but safely and uniformly, considered anathema. These specific atoms of content are to be excluded (or included), not because of any artistic necessity, but because of marketing needs: the negative need of not offending any group that will cause trouble for entrepreneurs and the positive need of attracting demographically defined and market-researched "adult" and "mature" audiences. The figures and fables of any mass-marketed and mass-manufactured medium thus manage to obliterate parochial differences while never challenging the narrow particularities of audience assumptions.

The legitimacy thereby conferred on human experience is narrow in range, with an emphasis on those emotions liable to help move along the action of a typical media drama (or news story): primary feelings that spring from simple conflict, particularly family conflict, and greed or lust. Rage, envy, courage, kindness are painted in vivid kindergarten colors.

At a time when the relatively limited number of vocational choices and social situations of bygone folk cultures has been transformed into the much richer and thus more frightening array of opportunities and dangers for members of the mass society, the media community presents a limited and remarkably unsuitable set of role models in its action-adventure, situation comedy, and melodrama formats. True, the regularity and predictability of these programs afford a release from the uncertainty of daily life. Everyone knows the characteristic way Steve McGarrett of "Hawaii Five-O," or Columbo, will solve a crime and deal with his suspects—themselves stock characters with stock emotions. There is comfort here, but there is tragic loss as well.

If folk culture with its tales could legitimate the limited set of emotions the child would experience and thus could integrate him into the community; if literature could expand the horizons of the adult to see and realize the almost infinite gradations of feeling that life might provoke, then popular culture might try to expand the emotional range of its characters to meet the varied and unexpected situations of the conflict-teeming life of mass society in transition. Unfortunately, formats and market necessities do not permit this, so that we are left with either vaudeville hostilities vented in slapstick or factitious preachments of brotherhood clumsily attached to melodrama.

The folk community was one of time-bound tradition, slow moving, with each motion affecting the whole. It was organic. In this light, the media community is hardly the global village that McLuhan hoped for, nor the instrument of the new nöosphere, the electronically neural net of man's mind enveloping the earth that Teilhard de Chardin saw as in a vision. The media community is made up of atoms. The audience is a collectivity of market-research numbers. The programs, the stories, the series, the events, all the output of the media are modular monads that can be plugged in to appropriate time slots, a notion of time alien to community but at home in the factory. Information and news are transmitted in bits, atoms of knowledge, with no past and no future, but alive with a kind of instant exchange value, a ghastly form of the mental money that makes up current communication transactions. *Time* makes everything more interesting, especially its readers, simply by serving up bits and pieces of entertainment and information already packaged in presentable chatter form, for exchange at a party of strangers who have nothing in common but the wires that keep them connected to the media community.

ten
The End of Obscenity

The power of Mediaworld to transform consciousness into an instrument for modernization through mass culture is easily seen in the transformation of the tribal concept of obscenity into the marketing category of pornography. Obscenity is the result of a conclusion, felt rather than reasoned, from a cultural premise about what is clearly forbidden. It is the cognitive consequence of a taboo and a protection, as it were, for the integrity of the taboo.

In a culture that is not obsessed with mechanizing the human body with devices and chemicals, eating with the hands instead of a tool may be acceptable. Cleaning the anus with the hands may also be a common practice. It would stand to reason that eating would wisely be confined to one hand and cleaning relegated to the other hand, where scrupulous cleansing of the hands is neither possible nor customary. To eat with the left hand is taboo in many cultures only because cleaning the body with that hand is expected. To witness a person eating with the left hand (even though he might be a modern surgeon of virtually pathological immaculateness) would therefore produce disgust and fear, the common reactive combination obscenity provokes.

Incest between father-in-law and daughter-in-law in some

tribes had led to vicious blood feuds. As a radical protection against future blood feuds, they decreed that men could not even speak to their daughters-in-law. Such an overture would be considered obscene. The rules tend to be strict because sex as a passion cares not much for the larger public questions of the social arrangement even though the social arrangement, from private property to the succession of kings, depends very much on the outcome of sexual behavior. Fear of punishment as strong as the attraction of the sex drive has long been deemed necessary to preserve general order at the expense of personal happiness, or at least at the expense of transitory and subjective convictions about the conditions for happiness.

Although there exists a wide variety of taboos and thus a wide variety of what may or may not be considered obscene, nevertheless every cohesive society does have some notion of the obscene that is a function of its rules about sex and hygiene —arenas of behavior where control, from the folk point of view, is of paramount importance and thus also fields where desire and fear contend.

Modernization, with its bureaucracy and technology, has wrecked folk cultures on a worldwide scale to such a degree that modernization (for the most part Western industrialization) could almost be defined as "defolkification." Mass media are often called the eyes and ears of the world; more aptly, they are the mouth and tongue of modernization, whether capitalistic or state-socialistic, directing their techniques to the conscious undermining of folkways wherever they are believed to retard industrial progress.

As a wondrous machine of marvels, a film projector or a television receiver is a powerful persuader of the virtues of modern technology. As a window on a world of comforts and spectacular diversity, any program that merely shows the surface of any modern city is a powerful argument for leaving the farm. Many years ago internal Russian propaganda showed a film clip of a black being beaten by Chicago police during a race riot. The intended effect, that *Amerika* is a land of cruelty and repression, was lost on the soviets. Beatings they were familiar with, but how did such a lowly peasant merit such magnificent shoes, well displayed by his prone position! Modern media argue for modern goods without regard for social consequences.

Beyond this structural and unconscious bias of modern media are the calculated uses of media messages and propaganda techniques to destroy folkways that impede material progress and the march of modernization among backward peoples. The New Deal of President Franklin Delano Roosevelt commissioned brilliant propaganda work aimed at the American farmer, whose backward ways, it was believed, created the dust bowl. Par Lorentz's *The Plow That Broke the Plains* and other "documentaries" of surpassing artistry argued for the inevitability of methods we now associate with agribusiness, and for the superabundant virtues of electrical power. Meanwhile, in the U.S.S.R., a series of boy-falls-in-love-with-collective-tractor films were urging (with less success) the introduction of higher technology and more complex bureaucracy throughout the steppes and Siberia. Today, in South America, Africa, and India, modern media utilizing satellite transmissions are bombarding the folk of the Third World with "training" and "educational" films on how to farm, how to build, how to limit their families, how to practice modern hygiene, how to eat more nutritiously.

In short, as modernization moves in on traditional societies the media community and mass culture—Mediaworld—replace folk culture. As the factory and the single cash crop disperse agricultural villages, tribal or class consciousness is gradually erased and mass man makes his appearance as a unit of production and consumption, urged on to greater feats of both by continual media messages. He sees himself more as an individual with a personal history, paradoxically just when his biography becomes less particularized by a local way of life and more resembles a statistical unit common to almost the entire globe.

He is personal in the sense that he is no longer tribal; his actions are his own, without the complex familial and clan relationships that suffocate, even while they support, the individual. Seen from the point of view of the educated and relatively affluent individual, who can afford the professional (and thus technological) support systems of modern medicine and counseling and the luxuries that abundant fossil-fueled power can bring, the folk are irremediably benighted and provincial. In the mobile America of the thirties and forties, and still of today, the virtues of folk life are seen as the vices of lower economic status and isolation from the mainstream of economic and educational opportunity.

With the mad logic of the machine that cannot be turned off, however, the benefits of industrialization and modernization are gradually choked off by the very proliferation of the system. The fear of hospitals and highways that tribal folk had to learn to overcome as a form of ignorance has returned to their descendants as a form of belated wisdom: ecological concern and anti-bureaucratic animus are both pre- and post-modern. The folk concern with sexual rules and consequent sanctions against culturally defined obscenities are beginning to return in the form of concern for personhood and equality among the sexes. Modernization and the consciousness of the media community begin as detribalization but inexorably go on to create a depersonalization far more undignified than the ignorant sacrifice of the individual maverick or genius to the stability of the clan. The pressures of the tribe were to make one a part of a living whole, but a human one. The pressures of the mass modernization machines are to make of the individual a unit— a depersonalized unit. In fact, lack of personal animus is a virtue in modern society: Often one individual will inconvenience, or even physically damage, another individual with the offered (and accepted) excuse, "I am only doing my job."

Depersonalization and lack of intimacy are cliché characterizations of modern social life. Discontent with these well-documented and amply-experienced marks of our time has created what Kenneth Rexroth has noted as an "instinctive revolt against dehumanization." Ironically, however, the instruments of consciousness revision, the media, are structurally tied to the machine model of input-output, and all the characteristics of the transitional forum of public opinion and of mass culture, which it serves and serves up.

This maddening cul-de-sac is best seen in contemporary treatments of the question of obscenity. It is rarely treated, in the media, as a culturally functional concept. Obscenity is rather seen from the point of view of a collectivity of isolated atoms, each seeking its own good in its own way. Obscenity thus becomes a totally subjective matter of taste.

The economic and political arrangements of the modern world are not matters of blood and soil. To think of them that way would be a fearful atavism. Rather, the arrangements of property and work, and therefore of meaning, are through rationalization, through highly abstract orchestrations of technology and bureaucracy. The personal is that which is outside the system. Sex has nothing to do with the social order in the official view of the modern bureaucratic liberal democracies. It is a matter of persons dealing with their own limited time. It is emotional. It is private.

There are of course a variety of laws governing sexual behavior, but these laws are seen more and more as holdovers from a folk society, which indeed is exactly what they are. Recently, a woman in New Jersey was charged with a crime of fornication. Her lawyer, with weary confidence, moved that the charges be dismissed since the law was an outmoded product of the fear of illegitimate births and social diseases. The judge informed the lawyer that two of the most overwhelming social problems of the time (1975) were illegitimacy, with its attendant anomie, and a virtual epidemic of social disease among teen-agers.

Culturally, of course, in modernized society, these problems are separate components. Private freedom from government interference, as we naïvely understand it in the transitional forum, demands that no legal sanctions be taken against private acts of sexuality—private being understood in the strictly physical sense of outside of public observation and without legal or official status. Social conscience, on the other hand, dictates that we deal with illegitimacy and social disease through appropriate impersonal technologies of medicine and public education, providing money enough for both as systems in their own right.

Having intensified the modern notion of the private as that which is left over after the public demands of the modern nation-state have been met, Mediaworld encourages as much enjoyment as possible for the isolated individual on his own time. This enjoyment, he is socialized to feel, comes from the acquisition of products that will solve his problems, giving him yet more time, which itself becomes defined as a problem of leisure, which in turn is solved by consumable products, and processes conceived of as products. Packaged tours, for instance, are convenient ways of making experience a form of product, which can be bought in a variety of "styles" and "sizes."

It is a logical, indeed an inevitable next step, to look on the human body as one more product, with sex as one more purchasable process, which can be looked on as a further problem to be solved by products which surround the process the way astronauts, and readers of *Playboy,* are surrounded by gadgets and chemical energizers and tranquilizers as they lie on their respective couches ready to deal with their respective technical challenges. Mass culture, with the inevitable logic of the market, encourages the natural tendency of a technological and bureaucratic society to see the body, and the bodies of others, as mere instruments of pleasure or pain. This mechanistic view finds its ultimate expression in the technical triumphs of the sexual-change operations and the heart transplant procedures, both of which replace, rather than treat, the most overtaxed parts of American go-getters and their worldwide imitators.

The sexually obscene, that which threatens a tribal taboo designed to protect a folk order, is totally without a locus of definition in such an instrumentally contrived world. The technology of the pill, abortive procedures, antibiotics and modern hygiene have formally eliminated for the affluent the worst of the physical prices promiscuity had demanded. The price remains for the poor and the ignorant, not yet served technical protection by the state bureaucracy, although the modernizing socialization of Mediaworld has all but removed the psychological restraint of the folk taboo.

Since it is social definition with its creeds and codes and cults that gives meaning to life, the absence of a public code based on a creed for sexual behavior has given freedom at the cost of meaning. What is left is what the media transmit best: short lessons in atomistic techniques for immediate, if trivial, results. Consequently, the media-fixated middle class is caught in a madness for method as a substitute for meaning. Sensuous men and sensuous women are not so much people who enjoy their senses, in this context, as they are dull students of instruction manuals on how to be carefree, self-centered, and eruditely narcissistic.

Folklore and folkways, the stultifying laws of the peasant, are, of course, not universally examples of earth wisdom that are flawless because unsophisticated. The point is that their destruction by modernization and their replacement by the mental modules of media lore are not examples of the march of civilization or the introduction of advanced science. Aphrodite has her dark side, but it is no sign of progress to drop her for Myra Breckenridge.

In promoting aimless rutting as a release from the rational

strictures of pointless and programmed jobs, the modernizing media are prescribing Bombay martinis for a nervous man with an ulcer. In transforming obscenity to pornography, Media-world exploits perhaps the most ready-made category of instrumental assumptions: progress. More is "permitted" now than was allowed to our forefathers, for whom, presumably, a glimpse of stocking was something shocking. This more lenient granting of permission is seen as progress. The salient analogy is that of the life of a child; as he grows older, more is permitted.

The analogy and the assumption behind it are maddeningly misleading and viciously patronizing. If more is "permitted," then there must be some central authority that has thought better of his or her previous, and presumably groundless and bigoted, restrictions. Such a view places all adults in the pose of perpetual children, who can look forward to ever greater "new freedom."

The argument of this book thus far would suggest a different explanation for this alleged progress toward more "permissiveness" as Spiro Agnew and *Time* call our pornography-prone condition. Mass culture must desensitize us to the situations that folk culture, in its organic need to preserve both itself and the values it gave to life, surrounded with a sense of moral responsibility. Pop psychology, distributed through the media machine, too facilely identifies moral sensitivity with neurotic guilt. If the body is an appended gadget to the will; if it is something that can be narcotized, destroyed, made hostile to new life, frozen and stored for future use, sexually altered, then it is an instrument, a thing.

Ironically, the assumptions of instrumentalism, in making immediate pleasure the sole end of bodily manipulation, have destroyed true sensuousness by destroying native sensitivity. In being tribal, obscenity had also been personal. The new freedom, as it is popularly misconceived, is just another way of introducing the impersonal and the dehumanizing into the realm of the private.

KITSCH AND CONTROL

Just as the marketing system of mass production, in its domination of the news and information business, has tended to reduce more and more forms of communication into formats for propaganda, so has the popular mass culture distribution and promotion system tended to shape and twist the genres of art into vehicles for kitsch. For if propaganda is a behavioral stimulus to get people to act without thinking, kitsch is a technique of reduction to get people to react without feeling.

From the viewpoint of the consumer, kitsch goes beyond being a verification of the familiar and becomes a confirmation of the nursery assumptions an unexamined life preserves. With his paperback mystery, his favorite television series, his accustomed media host, the consumer of kitsch knows exactly when to laugh, frown, coo, lean forward with interest, slump back in relief. Although media managers have a stake in keeping the audience passive and programmed, they could not begin to achieve the degree of success they have attained without the acquiescent, if not enthusiastic, complicity of the public.

Voluntarily, the habitual consumer of media kitsch is converting his leisure into another dimension of his labor. If his labor is part of a bureaucratic arrangement that makes workers interchangeable parts, units of input, greased and stroked by scientific Personnel Relations, then his leisure has become part of a vast bureaucracy of leisure management, the world of films and TV and radio and mass-marketed print, pulling and pushing him through each day, each week, each year.

With the proper advertising campaign, almost any low-budgeted film can be a very big hit. This was difficult to do in the past, but with block-booking and saturation advertising, certain "exploitation" films can recoup many times their cost in one or two weekends. Some films are not even made until audience research has discovered the appropriate market for them. This is particularly true of the 1976 spate of man-against-nature-

and-brother-to-wild-creature films, which are a kind of pornography for children and families. There is little plot, turgid dialogue, stock footage—all building to one Big Scene which has been promoted in TV clips and which children, programmed to anticipate the wild ecstasy of this scene, impatiently wait for. When it comes, they shriek with the delight that everybody has told them they will feel. They are learning early to fit into Mediaworld.

In its more extreme forms, kitsch becomes unbearably offensive as true pornography, through the technique of producing the bodily feelings of sexual love without any hope of human interchange, and indeed with the definite promise of no human contact.

The media community is thus a land where ideas and feelings are counters in a perpetual market of promotion and sales. Megalithic office buildings and cavernous assembly plants are but the front end of one long metaphysical production line, with Macy's and Sears—all the huge emporia of the nation—on the other end. Both ends of the line are peopled by diligent units, who work in three or more shifts, as producers and fabricators or as buyers and consumers. When they get away from the actual process, they are followed by the ever more efficient tentacles of perception that more advanced media can bring to bear. Radio and television are portable. A tent in the Maine woods is still only a switch away from what the real world has to say. The astronauts were treated to transmission of pro-football games in outer space.

The global reach granted the entire electromagnetic spectrum through satellite transmission and the delicate precision of audience-targeting created by computerization have combined to make the media community literally inescapable, unless one has the dedication of an anchorite. Even if practical problems created by overcrowding and pollution decentralize both production and consumption in the physical sense—industrial parks and landscaped shopping centers replacing discarded and wrecked cities—the media will keep the geographically dispersed masses psychically mobilized and narcotized at the same time.

High technology and advanced bureaucracy have given us more time away from jobs and from menial tasks and thus more privacy and more leisure. With symmetrical compensation, media technology and the bureaucracy of entertainment have plugged our privacy into a public world of leisure management that has made of our own time a task. The leisure world of America thus resembles one big store or county fair that never ends, with loudspeakers announcing where bargains and pleasures are for sale, and with crowds rushing to comply with the message. The media machine has enabled barkers to reach everyone wherever we are. To be out of reach of a sales pitch makes one feel as though he were out of touch with reality. No comment could be a greater tribute to the legitimating efficacy of Mediaworld.

The market management of the mass media has thus created and maintained a peculiar surrogate for lost community. It is vast in size and peopled by strangers. Nonetheless, these anonymous hordes follow the same adventures, feel the same sentiments, share the same calendar, celebrate the same events, absorb the same implicit instrumental values, select styles of appearance and styles in attitude from the same narrow palette, and are schooled to function as consumers of products in virtually every aspect of life. Mass culture has characteristics borrowed or adopted from high culture and folk culture, without the soul of either. It tries to provide the psychic support of folk culture without a local habitation or a history. It provides access to the artifacts of high culture while screening artists from their publics and obliterating the sense of irreplaceable particularity that until now has accompanied their enjoyment.

The media community has spawned a McDonald's of the mind: ubiquitous, yet fixed; multitudinous, yet unvaried; maddeningly inescapable, yet somehow comforting in a strange world. These marks of Mediaworld in America and the developed countries find their counterparts in the communication-sustained sense of community foisted on the socialist countries and on the Third World. It may be that the inescapable message there is to be a good worker, to pick up a hoe and take off that tie, to enjoy native rather than foreign foods, to sacrifice personal needs for the sake of the revolution or the fatherly leader. Willy-nilly, the dominant order, political or economic, infuses the technology of communication with its own life and tends to blanket folk cultures and drown out high cultures, while exploiting both.

There are, of course, other forces at work that are centrifugal. The very success of mass culture and industrialization has encouraged a nostalgia for folk cultures, or ethnic awareness, as Mediaworld has wisely sanitized it. But the logic of Mediaworld is for oneness, coupled with the potential for infinite repetition. These characteristics bring about an increase in consumption and in production, acceleration of pace of life, impatience with subtlety, positive hostility to leisure and contemplation, and a paradoxical stimulation of both envy and passivity at the same time.

The South African government, whose management of the black population depends on separatism and on promotion (with its attendant containment) of tribal culture, cannily postponed television broadcasting until 1976. The native whites, with one of the highest material living standards in the world, could no longer tolerate being left out of the media community. Now that they are in, their own fragile separatist world will be severely shaken. Whether the blacks will be any better off is a moot point—they will certainly desire more material goods and become more aware of their deprivations. They will be treated to the inexorable logic of Mediaworld, for good and for ill, as it adds one more province to its empire of consciousness.

The other world, the world that so many consider as the real world, is still out there. In this world of earth and sky and blood and flesh, still refreshingly, even terrifyingly, plural, there are hundreds of millions of our fellow humans who have been witnessing the deeds of Lorne Greene as a cowboy paterfamilias each week as they are now observing Jack Lord impose order without humor in Hawaii, a suitably polyglot non-place. When Americans have stopped watching the current action-adventure cycle and are on to something marginally novel, the Third World will be with the media form of the after-life, reruns.

Suitably mainstreamed for all fifty of the states and western Europe, many of these sagas are yet too culture-bound for true cosmic audience participation. Somewhere, it may thus be surmised, someone (with more reason for dedication than the old League of Nations or the United Nations could ever muster) is patiently drawing up a list, which may someday become a virtual law.

It will be called the Universal Production Code of Mankind.

eleven
Mass Addiction

Mediaworld is the mechanization, and thus the modernization, of the art and knowledge of mankind. Appropriately, Mediaworld is in the middle. It mediates the comfort and wisdom and gossip and tales of folk culture to a mass audience. It mediates the visions and creations of elites, multiplying and scattering the sharp bright seeds of individual genius to a multitude. In doing this, Mediaworld has transformed folk and high culture into something else—into something middling and mediocre.

Mediaworld, as we have seen, scrapes off the rough edges of local ethnicity from folk culture, seeks out the saleable center, polishes it to a high gloss, and markets millions of infinitely repeatable units. With the more specific and individual particularity of high culture, Mediaworld more subtly erases the special aura that Walter Benjamin saw surrounding every singular act of creativity and makes of it a type and model to be marketed: collections of Bach's greatest hits. The audience is kept on the alienating plane of the abstract, never feeling the bite of an individual essence. It is an atmosphere of attitudes that spreads to other experiences; families do not buy homes, they invest in real estate. News does not provide contact with the world so much as small change in the currency of mental money exchanged at meetings and parties. Feeling and thinking are newly subject to fetishes because Mediaworld has reduced art and knowledge to commodities.

Throughout this book attention has been drawn to the fearful symmetry of Mediaworld: the complementarity of modes of production with modes of consumption, the distribution of packaged issues and the collection of sanitized responses to questionnaires, the expectations of middlemen and the expectations of audiences. The moral dimensions of the symmetry become more evident in the context of mass culture.

Folk culture, as we have noted, was organic; mass culture is modular and atomistic. High culture generates a demanding atmosphere within which individuals can encounter the stubborn and irreducible facts of particularity, the sting of the specific; mass culture is a factory of assembled types, of predictable formats for fragments of life. Modish therapies and packaged tours both deal with the outer and inner world in the same way, through the formula treatment of abstract types: types of places, types of people, types of suffering. Unprogrammed ideas and unprocessed individuals, whole cultures and whole persons, cannot fit the marketing necessities that mold the media and the mass.

From Homer to Pynchon and Updike, literature provides a community of fully articulated reference points for feelings about unique yet universal experience. There is an enriching of the experiencing self in communion with other men, drastically different yet recognizable from within. The resultant legitimation of feelings transcends the folk and the time, but is limited to the human heart. In this world, a doctor can compare one's inner anguish to that of a mythical Greek king.

The mass media train illiterates in a narrow repertoire of stock responses to pre-packaged "situations," comic or melodramatic. Situation lives are fragments. Fellowship can be reduced to the snappy spirit of "Mission Impossible," "Mod Squad," "Switch," and "S.W.A.T." In Mediaworld, doctors teamed with popularizing wordsmiths can promise extinction of one's inner turmoil by reducing it to the result of a poorly played "game" or the assumption of an inappropriate "role."

Mediaworld must avoid the specific and singular and send out the typical and the general. We have already seen the marketing rationale for this necessity. In distributing stereotypes rather than creating archetypes, the media are not forming a very sharp or singular concept of the audience. For the format at one end is made for the target at the other end. If the stereotype is not art because it is incomplete and fragmentary, even while it lacks clarity and definition (the paradox of the banal), the mass audience, for whom it was crafted, is an equally blurry composite.

The artist writes for himself, and thus for everyone. The folk speak confidently within their own universe. The media are meant for the most, for all, and thus for none. The specific targeting of certain television programs, magazine advertisements, and new products for specified segments of the public only emphasize this blurring of the person. Specific targets are not specific people, but statistical segments, the stereotypes on the receiving end of the machine that prepares stereotypes for their consumption.

In tennis, in conversation, in lovemaking, we respond at the level we are addressed. If individuals are really not even being seen, if personal differences are invisible to media managers since they must deal with composite figures constructed by market research, if we then spend large fragments of our lives listening to their messages, we risk becoming what they wish we were—facilely manipulated and predictable units, atoms of purchasing power, with all of our needs created by advertising, rather than merely channeled through it, with our total curiosity confined to the marketed "issues" generated for our interest.

This personal distortion is the real danger of media immersion for the modern American. Without the ready-made grooves of folk or stable bourgeois society (and the price of resignation to a fixed niche that they exacted in turn), any individual is all the more dependent on Riesman's radar not merely to guide his actions but to actually define his identity. Media research has constructed a menagerie of statistical types that advertisers and programmers hail with blurred and unfocused broadsides. Specific persons are thereby reduced to general types, with no history (just number of years of school), no status (just income level), and no personal traits (just an inventory of possessions). If media messages, as we have seen, promote the notion that life is a series of problems to be solved by products, audience and readership surveys enhance that view by presenting people as the sum of their certificates and warranties.

In prison, in boot camp, at boarding schools, in nursing homes, in hospitals, the inmates are controlled by the way they are addressed: as numbers, as units, as clay, as disease. Personal identity is defined by the custodial and formational institution. Since terms of stay are limited in time and space, the definitions are only partial and only temporary. For some pathetic few, the total inmate, the "lifer" in whatever institution, benign or punitive, personal development has been pitifully warped and enfeebled.

Advances in technology, as we have noted, have given the media a global reach, and the economic system within which they operate encourages continual output. The amount of time Americans voluntarily spend mentally wired to the media is a major percentage of each day, as it is for every modernized and modernizing people. During that time, individuals become members of the mass, drawing their sense of themselves and of the world from the atomistic and sanitized packets of media messages. The "mass" is not so much a name for a group of humans, presumably deprived and depraved in some measure and none of whom has ever been met by a reader of this book, as it is a title for an activity performed by anyone, regardless of class, income, or prior years of schooling.

To avoid membership in the mass, one would have to use the media in a totally selective way, merely as a delivery system for a specific work of art, or as a quick headline service, without the illusion of being thus in touch with "what is really going on." The socializing comfort Mediaworld provides for the mobile and alienated American is so powerful a habituator that such usage is extremely rare. The media are like cigarettes: users are "a drag away from a pack a day."

In any given situation, the person *responds* at the level addressed. The person *becomes* the type *habitually* addressed. During any given week, the average American is addressed at many levels (another characteristic of modern urban life): as a person by an equal, as a client by a bureaucrat, as a target for a salespitch, as a set of given attitudes by a news commentator —as all of these things and as many more besides. But the most frequent, the least painful, the most expected, the most common and accustomed level of encounter for more and more Americans is a one-way interface with a machine that mediates a pre-packaged message, or bit of entertainment, addressed to the mass man. Further, as we have seen, the methods and formats of media messages are increasingly the model for face-to-face communication.

The mass is thus not a figment of the academic imagination, nor a necessary devil for cultural puritans. Since each individual in the eyes of God and in the strict scientific sense is unique, there can be no mass in the literal sense; no amorphous mob milling about the heartland of America, mumbling at station breaks, and gobbling up wire-service copy like some sci-fi monster. But the mass is nonetheless a very real characteristic of an entire population and, in the sense just explained, is becoming a dominant characteristic. The mass is certainly not another name for the lower classes or the uneducated; it is a name for what more and more people are becoming.

It is thus out of place to cast the high-culture/mass-culture debate in terms of economic class or in terms of group activity favored by different kinds of brows. It is a mistake to treat the difference between mass culture and high culture as a difference between rigorous high standards and a dismal failure to approach those standards. The universal reach and privacy of outlet that mark mass media in print and electronics have all but eliminated socioeconomic class as a factor in the debate. The media have democratized art downward, and *Dreck* upward, on the all-important cash scale of discrimination. If the media have shown *Macbeth* to legions of groundlings, they have also pushed "Mannix" through the mansion entrance.

Although necessarily blind to particular differences, mass marketing is nonetheless acutely attuned to socioeconomic class because of its relationship to purchasing power and buying habits. Mass-culture products and processes will therefore be priced, positioned, and promoted with exquisite attention to the statistical segment of the desired class the market manager has targeted. This precision has virtually no effect on the nature of popular culture or the artistic standards of the marketed object, as the following example should make clear.

Some years ago a synthetic substitute for shoe leather was developed. It had some advantages: it was waterproof, retained a shined appearance more readily, and resisted scuffing. It also had some disadvantages, centered around its inelasticity relative to leather. The marketing question was, "Who will want to buy shoes made from the synthetic?" There was debate on the matter.

The product could be presented as an exotic and sublime superior to everyday leather, and thus sold at a very high price to a market of relatively affluent people who wish to distinguish themselves, following the mass-marketed attitude, by the products they use. Alternatively, the product could be presented as a serviceable, no-nonsense substitute for expensive leather, with minimum care problems for busy people and thus sold at a cheaper price, but to a larger market. The point is that the material is the same, but it is marketed in a different style depending on the amount of money that can be realized by different strategies of sale. Merchandisers thus present the same material in different lights to appeal to different types of buyers, defined by the degree of their purchasing power. In essence, the rich and the not-so-rich are both being subjected to a polished salespitch that concentrates on imagined qualities of the buyer rather than the real attributes of the product. Virtues imputed to the buyer are seen as being expressed through the purchase of the product. In either case there is a leveling of differences to the lowest common denominator of shared stereotypes.

One statistical segment of the American public, suburban parents of young children with a mode income of about $12,000 a year, was shown to be ready for market-tested films that would be safe for their children, not require a trip to the central city, and be seen on the weekends. These films were specifically manufactured to meet the needs of this group and advertised heavily on television. (These are the Boy-and-Girl-Meet-Man-with-Grizzly-Bear films of 1976, referred to earlier.)

Joseph Heller's very successful book *Catch-22* was translated to the screen some years ago by Mike Nichols, who by that time had already achieved a very large market success, *The Graduate:* the winning formula of a best-selling book brought to the screen by a best-at-box-office director. Nothing can be left to spontaneous reception in mass marketing, however, and one of the most astute film promotional agents in the world was engaged to further guarantee future success. The question asked was similar to that asked about the leather substitute. Where should this product, whether great art or not, be positioned? *Catch-22* had been a book very popular with college students. *The Graduate* had been a film particularly successful with college audiences. The preview of the film, then, might reasonably be in a college town and perhaps academic superstars—the Washington Brain Trust–Harvard University constellation—might give the promotion of this film added luster with its chosen market. One of the first previews was given in Boston (not a film town) and many professorial superstars were invited. Before release, the film was a sort of delight of the intellectuals, and any segment of the market who wished to feel at one with the image of this group would be encouraged to see the film.

Among the marketing strategies cited, some were very successful and some were failures. The point is that the content, or substance, of the art, just as the nature of the product, is seen as a base from which to construct the ideal segment of the statistical audience for the maximum extraction of purchasing power by the marketers (not the makers, necessarily) of the product or the art. Once the choice is made, the promotional and sales messages concentrate on the personal lowest common denominator believed shared by the target audience and show how the product or art will enhance this characteristic, if it is positive, or diminish it, should it be negative. At both ends, the people and the art, there is a squeeze toward the middle. The art is either made for the masses or marketed for the masses. The audience is stereotyped into a mass in order to suit the chosen position of the product on the market. Although this or that particular strategy may fail miserably (from the Edsel to Ross Hunter's musical version of *Shangri-La*) the system as a whole succeeds and people, as a whole, are more thoroughly processed into masses.

Mass culture is thus measured by the distortion of the art and the distortion of the audience which the mass distribution system exacts from any given appreciation of any given creation in order to meet marketing demands. Mass culture is not some inert thing, lying about on the Jersey salt marshes, any more than the masses constitute a literal crowd of faceless humanoids overflowing real Levittowns. Mass culture is a daily occurrence, when a mass-marketed play or film or book or magazine or television program is delivered to a vast market of varied Americans. What are they doing that differentiates them from the connoisseurs of art, from the simple enjoyers of a good folk tale, from the direct experiencers of surf or sunsets?

It is not a difference arising from distinctions of taste, as though taste were a kind of continuum of trivial preferences from caviar to Dr. Pepper, with cost the discriminator. It is not a matter of class, as though fox hunting were more noble than boxing. It is not a matter of solemnity, as though black-tied auditors of *Eroica* cared more about what they heard than be-jeaned thigh-slappers in Nashville.

The difference lies in the nature of choice, in refusal to submit to routine, in pursuit of dialogue, in eagerness for surprise. Using media sights and sounds as a sort of blurred background noise to keep out the sound of one's own breathing is to be used by the media. Repetition obliterates judgment, slick presentation anesthetizes awareness, potential leisure becomes manipulated acedia. Seeking the machine-mediated bogus companionship of celebrities subtracts that much more time and pleasure from genuine companionship. News addicts, hungry for continuous news bulletins, deaden their sensitivity not only to the world, but to their own experience. Whatever the class or age or level of education, one becomes a member of the mass whenever one seeks a mindless connection to concocted propaganda for the head or contrived pornography for the heart. Addiction is the essence of the mass culture experience.

Addiction is the ideal form of product-customer relationship from the viewpoint of the supplier. If he can pay, the addict is the perfect customer: he never complains, except about himself, and he always comes back for more of exactly the same. More of the Same: the slogan of successful mass management—to use my original examples—from apples to hamburgers to TV series. All of the mechanisms of the market and the energies of media managers go into making media products, from issues of *Cosmopolitan* to episodes of "M*A*S*H" as regular as clockwork yet as urgently anticipated as the Messiah. As an experienced headwaiter is a master of patronizing deference, some media managers are consummate artists at attracting and holding attention without ever rewarding it. The socialized result of all this, *in globo,* is to reinforce the media as substitutes for the comforting rituals of folk culture, as we have seen. The individual result for the individual consumer can be quite paradoxical. His sense and his sensibilities become addicted to media messages, in almost the literal sense.

Chemical addiction is a mysterious process, although its paradoxical symptoms are notorious. Non-addictive use of anything leads to surfeit and subsequent abstinence, at least for a time, until a genuine need which can be served without any great sense of urgency recurs. It is rare to be addicted to water, though thirst, when the body needs moisture, can almost drive one insane. When the water is administered, the craving ceases, because the real need has really been served. Addictive craving for various chemical substances seems to meet no genuine physical need except that created by the administration of the chemical itself. In most cases, the more the addiction is served, the greater the craving becomes—it feeds on itself and creates its own hunger, at times unto death.

Perhaps because of our need for vitamin C, or some other cause now inoperative, humans seem to have a tendency for mild addiction to sugar. Processed-food marketers and Chinese restaurants put a good bit of sugar in a wide variety of their foods, adding a slight edge to the odds that people will buy the food again or at least feel hungry, strangely, after a full meal. Sugar is now recognized as a dangerous substance in the American diet by reason of its overuse. Seriously obese people or adult-onset diabetics can literally kill themselves due to sugar addiction.

More familiar is the addiction to drugs which change our perceptions and awareness or, in the canonized phrase, alter our consciousness. The paradoxical result of addiction is most dramatic here. Craving alternate consciousness, the addict virtually assures himself of a maddening monism, a cycle of constricting repetition that reduces the robust appetite for varied experience to a single fixation.

Everyone craves alternate consciousness: to see and feel things in a different way, to broaden the vision that one life confines us to, to cram the scant measure of our allotted time with event. Fiction, the making of alternate worlds, does this in part for us. Music and art, which compress and expand time, do this in part for us. Nonetheless, people also want stability. They want the comfort of habit and the solace of the parish. Undiscovered country, with its excitement, has its terrors. They stay home or hire a guide and see only his back. So few people ever really take chances; so few people ever really change their minds about anything important to them.

Accordingly, part of the appeal of drugs, even pedestrian drugs like alcohol and nicotine, is their capacity to cancel adventure and new enjoyment while seeming to promote it. Fearful of the risks of action, a person can distract his concentration with a drug. After a period of use, the person feels as spent and as euphoric as he might have had he done something, and the urge to achieve, to act, passes painlessly. Finally, feeling rather poorly, he has not the energy to even try to do something interesting and congratulates himself on the stamina and will power summoned up "to face (the same old) life" again, with the same old attitudes. Alternate consciousness has eluded not very serious pursuit.

Four to seven hours a day, seven days a week, winter and summer, the media addict gets through the year. He need never be alone. He need never see nor hear anything really different from what he has already heard and seen. He may watch the sons and daughters of the stars his parents watched go through weekly rituals; he may hear hours of bulletins that repeat and repeat, with the occasional mild spice of an "upcoming development"; he may eavesdrop on celebrities talking about themselves and not even have to shave or fix up the house to have them visit.

The greater group rituals of folk culture are replaced by private retreat to a favorite program: "No, I can't make it

Tuesday, that's when 'Honky and Son' is on."—"Don't feel bad, dear, have a warm bath and cheer up, tonight is 'Copper Capers.' "

Television news executives, who naturally wish their own programs to have more air time, know this habitual groove of the TV addict only too well. When a news program, on a monthly schedule, pre-empts a weekly series, or when a news special interrupts series programming, viewers not only do not watch (news specials have disastrously low ratings; that's why they have virtually disappeared from prime time in the last few years) but they are genuinely angry. Suggest to a ritual drinker that he skip a ritual cocktail for a swim, a stroll, or just about anything except a trip to get more ice, and he will become morose and peckish. Omit a program that is somebody's favorite, and domestic strife ensues. This may lead to the viewer version of solitary drinking: one's own set in one's own room —the media pursuit of loneliness.

Habitual readers of newsmagazines, newspapers and regular listeners to radio stations share TV-addict characteristics, although the addiction is less dramatically observable since their drug is more portable and not so rigidly scheduled. They share a brand loyalty, as it were, to ideas and art. Identifying the evening paper with slippers and pipe and easy chair, as Mediaworld has done for decades, could not have been a more effective portrayal of the mass plug-in. It remains, among the more recent variety of media forms and formats, the true tune-out (not in) and turn-off (not on) of the mass.

In sum, from the marketing viewpoint, addiction is the ideal attitude for the media buyer to have. Addiction has the paradoxical ability to inject urgency into a situation of monotonous regularity. The promotional hype that TV, newsmagazines, mass films, and other media give themselves reinforces this urgency in the consumer's mind. At the same time the delivered product is More of the Same—indeed, that is why it is sold and bought. A hard-drug addict is habituated to spending vast sums for his habit, even while it may be reducing his earning power. Mass man invests a large portion of his most precious commodity, time, in being processed by the bureaucracy of entertainment and the technology of opinion, even while he may be losing his ability and desire for true leisure.

The desire to experience art, the thirst for information, and the universal human craving for altered states of consciousness have all been focused, as we have seen, on media terminals, where packaged issues and formula dramas are delivered. Whereas boredom can be said to be a necessary precondition of civilization, the thirst for media ware has become a conditioned reflex that only leads to more boredom.

Étienne Gilson remarked that when he was a young man he imagined the man of learning to be one who walked about, as it were, in a formal garden which he had cultivated over the years, in total possession of each blossom, root, leaf, and twig. As Gilson grew more experienced, he realized that the analogy was very much mistaken. Growth in knowledge was more like a journey on a twisting mountain road. Not only did the higher land take on different appearances and shapes with the changing perspective of the ascent, so did the road already taken, seen from above. Nothing was possessed. Boredom and loneliness are the common hungers that may provoke the undertaking of such a journey. In Mediaworld, however, the potential voyager becomes a voyeur, imagining that whatever format he has been presented with is a form he has deeply felt.

Strange and exotic places, unheard of practices, rare melody, all are delivered to the media terminal in the custody of a host, a formula-familiar who neatly reduces the world to a one-minute wrap-up or a box of underlined highlights. The strange becomes a version of the familiar; the new, a certification of the (immediate) past. More often, of course, the terminals merely reprocess the already familiar formats of mass culture itself.

The desire to experience art is smothered by an overwhelming avalanche of kitsch. The desire for information is deadened by the cataract of News and Issues, the packaging of the unique events of the world into neat packets of routine categories. The craving for altered consciousness is channeled into media addiction, which feeds on More of the Same, with a paradoxical sense of helpless urgency.

It has been said that parents and old people now look to the young for understanding of the world and guidelines for behavior. The respect for older generations common to folk cultures is noticeably absent from mass culture. Margaret Mead attributes this switch to the rapid changes the world has undergone with a speed too swift for older people to assimilate. Experience of the past is no asset in a shifting society. Lack of experience, now viewed as freshness, is what the new forms of the new world require and which youth alone has.

There is also an alternate, and partially contrary, explanation. Without doubt the twentieth century has been a time of furious change, but one can make a case that since about 1914, let us say, any given individual may not really have perceived such a rapidly changing world. Tumultuous change has existed before—the French Revolution, the Reformation—without the reversal of youth-age roles being nearly so remarked. But since the turn of the century each passing year has seen our times increasingly dominated by the bureaucracy of entertainment and the technology of opinion and information marketing. These have formed the perception of each succeeding generation with greater efficacy. They have limited the scope of common experience more comprehensively to the formats of the media, while expanding the areas of coverage to virtually every aspect of life.

As mass culture has obliterated differences of place, Mediaworld has reduced the difference in times to the rubble of varied decades' pop styles (and has marketed this difference as "nostalgia"). Retrospectives about the century are totally dominated by media coverage of the past. History does not exist in Mediaworld. It is merely a morgue of Big Stories and Bygone Styles that can be dragged out for amusement or for packaging ("Another Titanic!") new events.

Age and experience in a mass culture, therefore, just mean more years of managed leisure and more exposure, in terms of sheer quantity, to propaganda, pornographic kitsch, formula drama, and packaged issues: Experience of repetition, more of More of the Same. Why should young people respect this accumulation of mental commodities? Further, old people were actually part of the Disneyland world of garter sleeves, oddly jerky movements, locomotives, Benjamin Franklin, Mussolini, Plato, and Eisenhower—a garbled waxworks of puppets without any specific place or era but that of the Bygone.

Desperate defenders of fundamental biblicism lamely suggested in the face of nineteenth-century evolutionary evidence that God, on one of the appropriate days of Creation, carefully laid down the geological and fossil evidence of prior ages and slow development, to give employment to geologists and paleontologists. Their naïve lack of scientific sense has been replicated by the ahistoricism of Mediaworld. Thus, only an imagination treated to Mediaworld could have dreamed up the recent science fiction plot, echoing the utterly other plea of the biblicists, that Intelligences from outer space created earth around 1950, complete with a storehouse of historical artifacts and artificially aged individuals with implanted false memories of a time that never was. To a media-attuned person, the idea is quite credible.

Brian Moore in *The Great Victorian Collection* has a museum full of everyday Victorian artifacts miraculously appear in a California parking lot overnight—a dream dragged into daylight. After extensive media coverage, the collection loses its interest and just fades away. J. G. Farrell, in *The Siege of Krishnapur,* has his Victorian defenders of the Old Raj erect an earthwork crammed with the quaint impedimenta of their time. It is an ineffective barrier against the barbarian attackers and gradually melts and rots into homogenized mud and junk. So does Mediaworld deal with the past, even as it uses it.

Voraciously gobbling up the art and artifacts and figures of the past as material for marketed leisure output, the media machine gives its users a false sense of knowledge. The country bumpkin in the big city, the eager youth newly come to the great university—these innocents of yesteryear were ignorant and naïve. Nonetheless, they brought large hungers begging to be filled. The children of Mediaworld, however, have already spent years as tourists of mass cultureland. Leo Tolstoy? "Yeah, the old Russian guy with the funny shirt and the farm who wrote about Napoleon and farming." They have been exposed to bits and pieces, without ever having absorbed the unique quality that only unpackaged contact with art can bring. Unfortunately, the bits and pieces have acted as a kind of spiritual vaccine against any fresh onslaught of unwrapped reality.

The technology of the modern media is capable of delivering, at a fraction of previous cost, a multitude of magnificent works of art, as well as eyewitness presence at great events (those few not yet staged for the media), to millions of individuals who are thus stimulated to seek greater direct experience of the world. Modern media can do this and modern media have done this as delivery systems. But modern media are overwhelmingly the tools of modernization. They are among the most capital intensive of all means of production. As such, the logic of the system requires that they be used every available minute by every available paying customer (paying directly or indirectly, through the passed-on cost of advertising). This need has spawned the bureaucracy of entertainment and the technological management of opinion and information. Together, these forces have created mass culture—by far the predominant characteristic of media use (granted, it is not the only use).

All habitual users of mass media are therefore reduced to the status of the mass man, immersed in mass culture. It must be emphasized again that mass culture is not necessarily a characteristic of socio-economic class. It is a characteristic of the production and consumption of products presented as ideas or art, stretched or shriveled on the Procrustean bed of marketing requirements. These requirements necessarily seek to multiply and standardize, thus removing the unique and the specific (the essential elements of information and art) from whatever they do, sending out signals that are general and vague. The consumers of the general and vague lose their own sense of particularity in the process, responding at the level at which they are addressed. Mass ideas and mass art thus live and feed on what they have created, the mass mind and the mass heart, anonymous and inert, yet ever in the futile motion of addiction.

twelve
Genre Ethics

We started out our investigation and construction of Mediaworld as the dominating and overarching structure which has set our cognitive style and the conditions for our climate of opinion. In doing this it has also made up much of our moral outlook, for the world we know is the kind of world we make decisions about.

The world, the non-self into which we are all thrown, has gone through different stages of development. First, the world was predominantly the world of the tribe and of nature: the world of physical work and the world of fixed social relationships among close kin. Second, the world became chiefly that of human artifacts and of the immediate family and institutional peers: the world of the city and of machinery, of the folks at home and of the gang at work or in school. Finally, we have what I have called Mediaworld: a structure of images and words manufactured for specific propagandistic purposes of marketing and manipulation—and one that overwhelms both the environment of work and the environment of the nuclear family. No historical development is globally uniform; astronauts and Stone Age food gatherers share 1977. But Mediaworld is the most widespread, most rapidly diffused, and most uniform of any historical stage because of the nature of the technology in which it is embedded: satellite transmission, computerized demographics, electronic instancy, mass duplication. The astronaut and the aborigine both listen to transistor radios and, as we have seen, to the same kind of programming.

Each of these stages of history, with its attendant cognitive style, has a characteristic moral and ethical world-picture. "Ethics" and "morality" have become thin, pale words in our time, stretched to cover everything from marital fidelity to laboratory protocol to car insurance. Yet, fundamentally, ethics and morality are the group-created and group-sustained rules of survival for a way of life and for life itself. Through some form of religion, richly ritualistic or austerely civil, these rules are internalized from infancy so that individual selfishness is checked at the source.

Sophisticated cultures have a moral code and ethical practices embodied in ideal types which become admirable and imitable for their own sake, for their moral elegance, as it were: the samurai, the gentleman. The fact that these ideal types sustain a total culture by motivating its members is not explicit, but is part of the "world" that is taken for granted.

As we have seen in our discussion of obscenity, the media are modernizing instruments that "defolkify," at times quite deliberately, the groups they are aimed at. As such, the media have a truly "demoralizing" effect as an ineluctable consequence of their modernizing function. As windows on a larger world, the media relativize any given tribe and hold its behavioral norms up for invidious comparison. This effect is the principal reason for censorship among totalitarian societies. But of course this kind of moral disarmament is not unique to the media. Trade and travel, conquest and economic cycles have long wreaked havoc on established orders.

I once met a young man, fresh from a small village in the Dominican Republic, at the small airport outside Ponce, Puerto Rico. For some reason he was trying to work his way to Venezuela. No doubt we perceived this same airport from opposite ends of the transcultural telescope. He approached me with a large old-fashioned pocket watch in his hand, the dust from revving propellers whipping his soiled trousers. He wanted to sell me the watch. He could see from my face that I was not interested and paused to marshal his most compelling argument, to quickly clinch the sale before I flew off. He said: "This is the watch that bus drivers use." His frame of reference might have been touchingly askew, but his angle of attack was authentic Madison Avenue. We were both in Mediaworld; I had merely arrived a bit earlier.

The media, by their structure, have a further and specific transforming effect on previously established moral orders. Before Mediaworld, history and tradition had always played a significant part in cognitive style and moral outlook. Generation upon generation celebrated their ideal types in song and story. Emulating the ideal meant joining a procession of illustrious prototypes and marching off, together, to a common future. (History affords a framework for activity and aspirations that is the intellectual and moral form of community.)

The bureaucracy of entertainment and the technology of opinion, the modern software devised for media hardware, are not concerned with history. Bureaucracy is concerned, without favor or prejudice, with separated and insulated procedures for narrowly defined compartments of life. The procedures may be parallel, like applications for a driver's license or a library card, but they are isolated atoms of disparate experience. High technology is compartmentalized too: the world of plug-in modules, of interchangeable parts, of total replacement rather than preservation through repair, of infinite repetition of identical units. Combined in Mediaworld, both bureaucracy and technology—the technocracy of mass culture—have given us formats for processing entertainment, and issues for organizing events and information. The media thus fundamentally alter morality and ethics, but not by invading heretofore separate cultures with outside images and competing ideal types. Rather, the media transform perception of the world by divorcing it from organic history, with its sense of place and time and familiar ideal types, and by breaking it up into separate components for isolated consideration.

This collection of separable components, equally characteristic of assembly lines, television schedules, and newsmagazine formats, is constantly extruded by the multi-faceted media machine into a steady flow of cultural jetsam and mental flotsam. As we have seen, it is to this constantly contrived flow that the mass is addicted. Such a stream of consciousness, played in the real world, makes any overarching sense of morality, binding on all men and women, psychologically inaccessible. Ethics and morality become incompatible with the cognitive style of Mediaworld because they are integrating and organic realities created over time by a true family of people.

The formats of entertainment and the issues of news-information create a mindset that is modernized in a radical way, marked by a schizophrenic discontinuity. Viewers and readers take on the psychology of spectators at a game, except that they are isolated from their fellow spectators. This of course is literally true of much of television broadcasting, which prominently features game shows, since they are so cheap to produce per hour of usuable videotape, and sports events, since production costs and facilities are in other hands. The psychology of a game is that it is isolated from life; it has a boundary, a fixed space and a fixed time, rules unique unto itself, with very clear and confined roles for different players. Formula drama and situation comedies share the same psychology, with stock characters in fixed frames of standard situations, reacting according to a limited repertoire of expected postures. News, following the set thematization decreed by news executives and market research, and packaged neatly in the pseudo-issues of the transitional forum, is also played before rank on rank of spectators, all schooled to follow the game. Both games and drama require spectators to suspend their disbelief, to accept for the moment the world of the stage, or of the field, as the world itself. The dramatization of news and the increasing use of formula-issues to package information introduce to the world at large the same confined world of the game which the media process for consumption.

Different games have different rules and different roles for players, with penalties for infractions. Street crime and rape is one game, with its rules and with its penalties. Suite crime, as white-collar crime has been called, also has its rules and its penalties, which differ widely from those of the body-contact sport of street crime. Professional ethics are still another game, with different rules and different penalties. Politics, considered by some the Great Game, has rules written and revised by the players themselves.

In the world of games, there is no such thing as personal responsibility. Whatever is done is done within the game. All action is relativized. There is no such thing as evil. There are only errors of judgment or bad plays, some of which, with the accepted capricious arbitration of sporting rules, are penalized.

Personal life is also seen as a game, and thus not as a sharing of a heritage nor as a chance to contribute to an ongoing tradition by emulating some ideal type in a contemporary yet faithful manner. One does not live, one assumes a "life-style." Each life-style has its own rules of the game and its own roped-off isolated area, or "scene." Whatever one does is according to a life-style within a defined scene. The style can be changed and the scene can be shifted.

Thus, quite literally, killing, cheating, lying, and stealing are redefined by taking them out of the common context of humanity and the historical context of a people with a code and a creed, and by placing them in the new context of a game. Killing is terminating with extreme prejudice. Cheating is achieving leverage. Lying is telling "our side of the story." Stealing is a transfer of ownership. Within the confines of any one context, any immoral act can be "accepted practice" and thus not subject to penalty, or even criticism.

Scandal and moral indignation are expressed when actions are taken out of the context of the appropriate game—as they would be, for example, if Walter Cronkite were to appear in overalls and love beads and put his feet up on the news desk. Thus, reporters are subpoenaed by Congress for leaking secret reports about American foreign policy and intelligence operations, revealing to the world, for instance, our abandonment of the Kurds to virtual extinction. The substantive horror, the callous sacrifice of an entire people to further "our interests" dubiously defined by unaccountable officials, escapes public scrutiny because the script has given it a minor role. A cabinet officer can survive with career intact, perhaps enhanced, despite intimate involvement with an international and national rape of the consumer and the taxpayer in a multi-billion-dollar wheat transaction. The same officer must resign when it is revealed he made a joke with racist import.

Mediaworld has in this fashion brought to birth a moral outlook, not to be confused with situation ethics, that I shall call "genre ethics." Situation ethics was a description for a serious effort to push principles into extreme hypothetical situations, in order to test their universal validity and to devise a hierarchy of principles emerging from conflict among moral imperatives. Would it be moral, for instance, to commit suicide if one were ill with a disease whose treatment was bankrupting one's family and subjecting loved ones to acute mental anguish? Such extreme cases bring to light subtleties of obligation and responsibility. But the genre ethics of Mediaworld are divorced from principle and responsibility, focusing on proper dramatic casting and on intrinsically consistent gamesmanship.

Mediaworld, with its constant flow of broadcast formats—self-contained monads of information and titillation—and with its cataract of print, neatly cut into atoms of well-tailored issues and personalities, has thus intensified the industrial and technological method of modular manufacture and has made of it a way of thought. McLuhan saw this kaleidoscope of material and considered it a mosaic of simultaneity, a seamless garment of perception which the viewer/reader organized by his "hot" involvement with a "cool" medium. What little study has been done on media perception and the experience of educators with media-reared generations does not confirm his sanguine interpretation. Bits and pieces are assembled as bits and pieces; so-called simultaneity has meant a lack of coherent organization; mere possession of disparate facts has been equated with knowledge.

Further, the literally fabulous increase of exposure to melodrama on a daily schedule, and the escalation of passive spectatorship, have created a mentality of suspended disbelief that amounts to a habitual attitude. If a sense of values and a hierarchy of principles—an ethic—does exist, there is no frame left to fit it. In the market, popularity is truth. Thus values vary with the frame within which they are applied. If a rock lyricist is enormously popular, then his words speak for a generation and his insights into life, his social criticism, must be profound. If market research shows that women are not particularly excited or turned on by glossy photographs of erotic male nudes in magazines, then *Viva* will change its format. "Family Feud" is a single television program which offers a total microcosm of Mediaworld. First, it features families and the familiar, the essence of the media community. Second, it is a game, a contest, between two ordinary families that are part of the audience. Finally, the families must guess answers to questions which in fact require no correct answer. The "right" answer is that which comes closest to what an opinion poll has shown to be the most common view, accurate or not.

Mediaworld thus breaks the world up into self-contained games and plots for which there are only local rules. Astronauts in Skylab, free from the gravity that binds us all to earth, found themselves without any sense of up or down in different rooms of the vast space vehicle. It was a most disturbing and frightening experience until they each, separately, decreed an arbitrary "local vertical." As long as each astronaut could work within the set of his own local vertical, there was no conflict. If two astronauts, in the same room, operated on different verticals, it was upsetting to both. Mediaworld, having come to birth in a time when the traditional forum with its universal moral gravity was dying out, has given people opportunities for constructing any number of "local verticals" relating to values, provided they stay within the same scene, within the same modular role. If you want to leave the narrow set, you must be prepared to shift values the way astronauts had to shift verticals.

Mediaworld, in its programming and content, gives to modern men a modular morality of local values. When this is understood, it is clear why so much of life is currently described in terms of roles played and games won or lost. For the Watergate schemers, CIA agents, the perpetrators of the Equity Funding scandal and of the wreck of the Penn Central, welfare chiselers and medical charlatans, are all playing roles in games that are perfectly in accord with the local vertical of accepted practice. "Nixon didn't do anything that other Presidents didn't do." It is only when Mediaworld, in its coverage, decides to shift scenes and recast the players that heroes become villains. They have not changed, but the set has. Kissinger is at this writing having difficulty adjusting to the new part the news and information business has assigned him. He was a hero, he was a villain; what he will have turned out to be when this is read is a matter not of ethics, but of drama criticism.

The presumptions of the Nuremberg Code, with which we punished Nazi war criminals, included the idea that there is one overarching moral code by which all men are bound. The presumption of the Nazi defendants was of a modular morality. Given the world of Hitler's Germany as the boundaries of the game, their actions were only accepted practice. In 1968, at the trial of Dr. Benjamin Spock for obstructing the military draft, the defense was denied an opportunity to introduce the Nuremberg Code on the grounds that it was irrelevant. Dr. Stanley Milgram's experiments, in which unsuspecting subjects were told to give severe pain to an accomplice of the experimenter (who convincingly acted out agony for the subject) on the grounds that it was a necessary part of a scientific experiment, showed that given the proper setting, enough people will play whatever rules of whatever game are established. Dr. Milgram also apparently felt justified in lying and seriously misleading his fellow humans on the grounds that it was necessary for scientific research—a reason not foreign to the defendants at the Nuremberg trials.

Two recent surveys, one of Ivy League students and the other of the general public, cast some confirmation on the prevalence of modular morality. The students felt that, given the historical circumstances, the German public could hardly have done otherwise than support Hitler, and that they (the students), given the same circumstances, would undoubtedly have acted similarly. In the other survey, given conditions of war, or of severe emergency, the general public placed the value of a single human life at $28,000.

Once again there is a fearful symmetry. As the propaganda style of media messages is matched by a protean public, so the genre ethics of media coverage and media drama are matched by the modular morality of the great audience.

Genre ethics are determined, like so much of media content, by the prevailing expectations shared by audience and middlemen about the proper role for public figures and (in true bureaucratic fashion) for types of occupation and status. On the one hand the favored position can be that prostitution is a victimless crime (implying that it is thus a "crimeless" crime) following a familiar scenario for the life of the prostitute not unknown to melodrama. On the other hand, a Utah Congressman can be unfortunate enough to have allegedly propositioned policewomen acting as decoy prostitutes shortly after a sex scandal involving another Congressman in Washington. This incident thus fits the same genre for Congressional immorality, as updated by the then current "issue" of Capitol Hill Follies, whereby extramarital sex is both hypocritical and sexist. If only a prominent rock star had been busted for drug use by undercover narcotics agents, if only a gifted and celebrated homosexual had been "entrapped" by anthropoid police methods shortly before the Congressman's interlude with the policewomen, he might have been cast as a victim of police-state tactics—or perhaps of "sexual McCarthyism."

An astute awareness of genre ethics is an invaluable endowment for a public relations firm. Casting their client in the most sympathetic role, by suggesting an appropriate scenario that might serve as the "handle" for coverage, gives excellent protection from damaging publicity, whatever the facts. Conversely, being assigned a villainous role virtually rules out fair treatment or favorable coverage. In classical rhetoric, it was said that he who defined the question won the argument. In Mediaworld, he who assigns the roles controls public reaction. Praise and blame are assigned to the appropriate featured players, to the roles. Inner conscience and real responsibility can only be portrayed in fictional drama.

If history and tradition are necessary for a sense of morality and ethics, then a sense of the enduring and growing self is essential for a sense of responsibility. Current attitudes to character and guilt and merit, however, are as destructive of the idea of the perduring self as modular morality is of a persistent code. Just as public figures and types are placed in set scenarios by Mediaworld, private behavior is broken up into disparate and atomistic modules, the "games people play." A character or personality is merely the sum of its good or bad habits, each of which can be dealt with separately and modified by behavioral methods. As the age is fragmented, the self is cut up. Ideals and long-range goals are meaningless in this setting; there is only the "feeling good about yourself" reward that is the "pay-off" for a properly played game. Point, game, set, match: game, role, scene, lifetime—human experience is stamped into separable modules, self-contained, without past and without future.

It may be that some sense of organic time, of the time of seasons and years, of mythical past and mythical future, giving a cosmic frame to the present moment, is a necessary condition for a sense of morality and a sense of responsibility for others and for oneself. Christopher Lasch has indicated that a lack of concern for posterity leads to narcissism. And certainly the current plethora of self-administered mini-therapies to help us feel good about ourselves has all the marks of narcissism. Certainly self-serving politicians who buy votes with libelously labeled social programs, paid for by promissory notes of money sure to be printed in ever greater quantities, are narcissistically hypnotized by the present.

Responsibility in Mediaworld is legally assigned, never morally assumed. Immorality in Mediaworld, locked in the present moment, is what an effective majority of contemporaries, either customers or voters, object to for whatever reason. The codes of the film industry and the television and broadcasting industry are direct results of objections on the part of contemporaries. They are methods of avoiding immediate trouble with a present market. The codes are also an example of the specialization of ethics. The codes are administered by executives and full-time staffs. The administrators are not philosopher kings or moral theologians, nor are they expected to be. They are in the public relations business and they are assisted by expert legal advice. Their task is to keep the public at large, and special interest groups, from interfering with the normal functions of a very large set of corporations with international markets.

In Mediaworld, morality is a specialty with its own bureaucracy, leaving others to get on with the real work of production and distribution.

The result of this specialization and the social outlook which produced it is that morality and ethics are even further removed from being the integrating norms for behavior that they once were. Morality is just one more "game" or "scene" for which there is a definite bureaucratically defined boundary, within which experts and specialists play out their assigned and predictable roles. Virtually no activity is seen as immoral in itself, although it may be offensive to the sensitive, insulting to women, demeaning to homosexuals, a slur on our military, alienating to the Jewish vote, unfair to native Americans, or some other objectionable quality in reference to a definite group with some clout in the marketplace or at the ballot box. Morality also becomes thoroughly objectified as a political aspect of behavior, and is removed from the realm of conscience and obligation, of intrinsic duty to a code and creed based on a heritage. The overwhelming numbers of contemporary members of Mediaworld simply outvote the daily diminishment of the dead, in a new kind of tyranny of the majority that John Stuart Mill did not foresee.

The absence of a binding and internalized moral code, the loss of tradition, and the lack of any hopeful vision of the future are signs of secularity. Harold Adams Innis, the Canadian communications scholar, saw a pattern of incremental secularization with each progressive step in what he called more "space-binding" media. In *Empire and Communications,* a work now well over twenty years old but still most provocative (and difficult), Innis traced the interplay between political arrangements and the dominant technology of communications at different stages of history. Earlier technologies were primitive and were bound to time and tradition simply because of the nature of the medium. Stone tablets are cumbersome to use and almost impossible to transport. As a result, this early medium did not encourage extensive records or distant travel, favoring an oral culture of parochial cults riveted to the past and hostile to material change. Later media were lighter, easier to use and easier to move. Paper made true empire possible by providing communication links over vast distances, a convenient form for official archives, and extensive and flexible methods of storing business records. These concerns weakened preoccupation with the distant past and reverence for "sacred" (because rare and strange) texts. Later lighter media were thus "space-binding" and were almost inevitably connected with secularity.

Innis did not extend his analysis to television and radio, but James Carey has related the paradigm to broadcasting. Television is the most space-binding medium imaginable when coupled with satellite transmission. It blankets the globe with the speed of light. But it transmits oral-visual messages, not the impersonal and secular printed word. As a result, Carey indicates, Innis's theory cannot be purely applied to the most modern media, since they mix his pure categories of space-binding and time-binding. On the one hand, television should hasten secularity because it is space-binding. On the other hand, it should cause a rebirth of religious feeling, or at least of decentralized, less imperial, political arrangements, because it is oral-visual.

I feel that Innis was essentially correct about the significance of the march of communications technology, and that the medium he did not have time to include, as part of a mix of many media working in concert, has produced the ultimate in secularization, or, as I prefer to think of it, modernization. I hasten to add, however, that the secular Mediaworld is not the ineluctable concomitant of the physical nature of the modern media, but rather of the economic system which they serve. China has a strong moral code, brutally internalized, and a clear vision of a collective future, based on a very long tradition. This civil religion had a Caesarean rebirth, with extensive propagandistic employment of modern media which can serve any master. Japan, far more modern and business-oriented, studded with television stations and multimedia markets, is facing a crisis of secularization, although it was never religious in the Western sense.

Others might disagree with this admittedly unprovable position and maintain, probably with McLuhan, that television creates heroes and makes legends live again, very similarly to the ancient oral cultures—citing the Camelot-cult of the Kennedys from the early sixties and the current extensive use of television and other modern media by fundamentalists and evangelists, as well as by fringe cults such as that of the meteoric Reverend Moon. This, I would argue, is to misread the response these men have created and to underestimate the distorting power of Mediaworld. For a limited number of followers, there are ecclesiastical superstars, who fulfill the role of entertainers, not leaders, saving the saved. Paradoxically, the spectacular overkill of media exposure has made most people numb to "charism" even as it is in demand. Once again, mass addiction is an antidote to the very conditions it seems to promote. Religious fervor, moral commitment, a sense of community—all require active participation of real bodies in real contact. Television audiences are vast, but they consist of isolated atoms. The mass media give only the illusion of participation through intimate electronically-induced pseudo-presence. In providing this substitute, they make it all the less likely that true commitment will occur, *pace* the mobs generated for spectator events like the Superbowl. Community is inspired by live occasions of self-generated festival, and community is only sustained by a constant creed, code, and cult shared by families and friends among a larger public. It is a living oral culture, not a museum of taped messages. Without a doubt, there is a genuine hunger for real values, true morality, and sustaining tradition. But in keeping with the very secular notion of salvation-through-purchased-product, we are beginning to see a bogus concern for "values" and "ethics" marketed as packaged programs in schools and in corporations. Following the modular morality of Mediaworld, the concern follows an issue, Watergate-cum-corporate-corruption, and will be administered by specialists in morality and values. The source of specific tenets about moral obligations and ethical practices will be solicited from those paying for the moral-uplift service, with sound market-research methods followed, including the employment of surveys and "in-depth" interviews.

At any time other than our own, such procedures would be considered ridiculous, if not contemptible. Before Mediaworld, art held the mirror up to nature and could show men what was outside themselves in ever new and refreshing perspectives. Mediaworld *is* a mirror, but it reflects back only what the majority is presumed to want—More of the Same, versions of its own image.

For the moment, the previous worlds of tribe and work, of made things and shared primary experience, have given way to the factitious images of Mediaworld. As they pass away, the notions of morality and ethics that they engendered, and above all, the notion of *truth,* the core of honesty and art alike, go with them.

Varied as they were, philosophers of the Classic period up until Descartes by and large tended to see the human mind as brilliantly passive in the face of nature. Men read the great book of the world, whether it was written by God or by blind chance, to discover truth. Some may have felt the text spoke clearly and simply. Others may have despaired of construing what would remain inaccessibly mysterious. But whether attainable or not, truth was there; it was real. Varied as they are, philosophers of the modern period up until today tend to see the mind of man as creative and constructive. Individual great men, or anonymous generations of men through the heritage of their language and culture, project visions on the blank screen of outer emptiness. Some may feel that the visions are of sustaining beauty and power. Others may feel that the visions are pathetic and ultimately pointless exercises in ego-defense or self-justification. In either case—and they are poles apart—truth is achieved, not found. For ancient and modern, realists and idealists, truth was important and central to human concerns, however conceived.

In Mediaworld, as we have seen, mercantile instrumentalism predominates. Ethics and morality are specialized tasks for human relations engineers. Truth is just one of the games people play. At times it is more effective propaganda than clumsy attempts at deception. Truth is still dangerous, however, and that is why dealing with it has been delegated only to the specially authorized. They are not philosophers.

part three
BEYOND
MEDIAWORLD

thirteen
Good Reception

In the early sixties, C. S. Lewis attempted what he called an *Experiment in Criticism.* He noticed that virtually all literary criticism was of the work—the book, the play, the poem —as though it were a thing complete in itself. But of course literature is not that at all. It is a process; it may even be a procedure. It is a living activity that begins with the writer's recording his thoughts and feelings through writing. The completion of the record is by no means the end of literature. The record must be read by readers and that act is the symmetric complement of the writer's writing—writer and reader are matched like dancers, although the writer is unquestionably the one in the lead.

Lewis therefore set upon the novel task of criticizing the *reading* of a work, the true end of literature, as an index of its worth. To do this, he had to be rather precise about what he meant by reading. He did not mean the mere physical act that is equally provoked by maps, menus, newspapers, dictionaries, and poems. He meant the mental, the spiritual, act that was the human reaction to art reached through words; the same act, in its way, that accompanied listening to music and gazing at paintings. Lewis had standards to apply to the proper type of reading for works of literature, and he chose to call the type of reading he approved of *receiving*. The type he felt was not appropriate for literature he called *using*.

In the end, Lewis felt that a book could be called good if it invited, or even only permitted, *receiving*. A book could be dismissed (as literature, as art) if it prohibited *receiving*. Such a book could only be *used*.

For cognitive psychologists, the act of perceiving reality is as constructive as any act of positive expression. Recognizing the letter A in various forms, as George Miller indicates, is parallel to writing the letter A in various styles. For Lewis, receiving is what others would call a creative act.

Receiving is the act of escaping the self and the narrow necessities of the moment in the very act of seeing another world through the borrowed senses and shared imagination of another human being. It is a coming together of empathy and insight, without a trace of self-regard. It is a special form of Plato's Wonder, the mark of the naïve philosopher in awe of the basic matter of human awareness. Receiving is the naïve act of living another's shared Wonder, transfused through art. Receiving, like Wonder, is always of something particular and concrete: *this* grief or joy or rage or heartbreak, and no other, is a common apprehension of the sharing self of the writer and the receiving self of the reader.

Once the self is discussed, the paradox of selfhood darts elusively through the argument. The self is never more itself than when it reaches otherness. The naïve immersion of the self in the ocean of otherness that literature and art provide gives growth and vigor to the knowing and feeling faculties of the self. For the receiver, as for the very young child, experience of art is revelation, not repetition. But if one reads or listens or looks or feels *in order to* become informed or cultured or sensitive, receiving becomes using, like taking a pill.

In direct experience, in life, the same paradox is felt in the common experience of being self-conscious. Self-consciousness is primarily consciousness of others' reactions to ourselves. Intent on others only as mirrors, we fail not only to see who is out there, we also fail to be ourselves. Simple apprehension of the utterly other is the greatest affirmation of mature selfhood. Once the reflection is ignored, mirrors become windows.

Using is merely the act of following one's own habits, staying within one's own needs, keeping one's own viewpoint, while exploiting someone else's words (or sounds or sights) to reinforce what is already within us. The reader has an axe to grind or a bubble to blow, and the book is mere fuel to turn the wheel or power the pump. Lewis does not condemn *using* as such, he merely points out that what is *used* cannot be *received* and that what cannot be *received* cannot be literature. Those who read to cultivate and prolong erections or to focus on prayerful devotion may be doing good or evil, depending on your view, but whatever they are doing, they are not *receiving* literature.

The person who unself-consciously revels in the click of the perfect golf swing, or in the ineffable flow of being "on" in a basketball game, when every intricate play seems inevitable, is first cousin to the *receiver* of literature. The cyclist who feels his pulse to make sure he is elevating his heartbeat to the recommended maximum, without a thought to the rush and rhythm of his road, is *using* sport for exercise. In short, literature is a world of experience; it is not a collection of instruments.

Knowing what Lewis expects of the reader, one can infer what he demands of the writer: the direct delivery of simple otherness, without the self-conscious worry about how he will be classified and without the explicit intention of producing an effect. The maker of literature, for Lewis, is captured by the particular grief or joy, the particular sound of rain or slant of sun, he is trying to share.

The pornographer and the propagandist are riveted on the reader, their object, not their subjects. They seek to "turn him on," to get his money, his vote, his cooperation. Instead of the dance of art or learning, the fearful symmetry of mutual exploitation unites reader and writer, audience and producer. Nothing is received.

Although Lewis restricted himself to literature and scrupulously avoided any moral judgment on *using* literature, his moral position is clear enough from the tone and context of his *Experiment in Criticism* and certainly from his many other writings, which form a coherent corpus of integral moral sensibility. For him the lack of ability to appreciate the otherness receivable through literature is a mark of narrowness, a sign of a suffocated self. Whether he is such due to circumstances or conscious choice, the user is less human than the receiver.

It must be granted that the media provide extraordinary occasions for receiving. Sensitive cameramen have unobtrusively visited tribes in New Guinea and hunters in the Arctic. Brilliant artists have been given the technical means to recreate past periods vividly with fresh and vital versions of great plays and great novels. The miracle of the electronic distribution of film and tape has brought to millions the Mountains of the Moon, in Africa and in outer space. These occasions, and others, have been extraordinary—and they have been rare.

As we have seen, marketing formulae necessitate routine predictability provided by the media bureaucracy; the eye of the producer is clouded over by visions of researched audiences. Virtually every mass-marketed bit of entertainment or piece of information is intended for a crowd that is automatically presumed to be made up exclusively of *users.* Anything new must be wrapped in the familiar and reduced to the routine.

This fear and caution, raised to an art form, pervades the public communications of educators, religious leaders, statesmen, and scientists, who have learned to imitate the style of sales presentations.

The sky is dark. With twinkling increment, it becomes peppered with stars. Finally, the Milky Way washes the heavens from horizon to horizon. Suddenly, an immense white square appears, then another, then a third, covering half the firmament. They are three panels from Charles Schulz's "Peanuts." Over the sound system, the voice of the star of the strip, Charlie Brown, thunders through the planetarium. The public has been saved from uncomfortable awe once more by another pre-fabricated verification of the familiar.

Such presentations are not merely patronizing; they are also a positive prevention of creative reception on the part of the audience, who are conceived of as respondents, potential buyers, restless and exhausted workers—statistical segments of programmed reactors to programmed material. *Use* is thus systematically preferred over receiving. The great paradox is that the technology of modern media, so fraught with promise for widening the world of actively receptive readers and viewers and listeners, has been carefully castrated by the crippling restrictions of marketing formats. Further, we have seen that the media provide a polished and professional collection of substitutes for community figures and institutions. They have replaced the personal with the mechanical and the programmed. This has reduced the need for the audience to react, to be active, to respond in any way at all. Viewers can pass out in front of Johnny Carson and he need never know.

It may seem a bit puritanically captious to apply Lewis's experiment to the media, when he was concerned with literature. After all, he would not find fault with Superman for not being Oedipus. Nevertheless, both the critics and the proponents of Mediaworld judge it for its ability to bring the great world to the small world of the home; the mass media are distribution systems for the many; accessibility is their principal characteristic. But the methods of media transmission, which have increasingly been imitated by other channels, such as the schools, the libraries, the churches, are designed to disinfect the differences, the otherness, from the message so that it can be blandly assimilated without resistance and without irritation. *Receiving* requires full attention to the particularity of the art —its difference.

In parallel fashion, information is mathematically catego- rized as the improbable, the unexpected, the surprising. The more anticipated a message is, the less necessary it is because it carries little information. News, by its very nature, is new; it is revelation of the previously unknown; it is unfamiliar. But the technology of opinion and the news business must process and organize news according to pre-sold headings, "the issues," as we have seen, thereby eliminating the element of surprise and the essence of news itself.

The bureaucrats and technicians surround the artist or jour- nalist at one end of the media transmission belt, as it were, just as they overwhelm the solitary target of the media messages at the other end. The procedure converts anticipation of the new to resignation to the usual. The unlikelihood of the mass being able or willing to *receive* convinces the producers to avoid the effort of originality. The unlikelihood of originality confirms the audience in an attitude of dull *use* toward whatever is transmit- ted. As Young Turks at all-news radio stations are fond of jibing: "In the next half hour, more of what you just heard in the last half hour."

From the point of view of the consuming audience, the media characteristic of predictability can be seen as a necessary and excluding alternative to the receivable particular and original, providing an escape not from life, but from art and thought.

Although it is unintended, there is ultimately a moral effect on the audience. It has little chance to exercise the latent faculty for *receiving;* it is continually reinforced in the habits of *using.* The media, the so-called eyes and ears of the world, are more like vast sets of sophisticated mirrors and echo chambers, send- ing back to the market-researched audience what the managers imagine the public wants because it is another form of what the public is.

fourteen
The Politics of Acceptance

The moral condition created by the media is fundamentally a question of politics. Propaganda and pornography are the end points toward which all forms of modernizing communications media tend. Acceptance of the pre-programmed module, as well as its manufacture, is a moral decision about the exercise of freedom. Purchasing mass-produced capsules of entertainment-information is surrender to a definite form of government and a choice of a type of community. No one can avoid community. One can only evade responsibility for the type of community he or she lives in.

Most people accept modernization or at least are resigned to it. The process of organizing life around industrial manufacture, high technology, detailed specialization, dense urban living, and the practice of relegating decisions to a bureaucracy are arrangements toward which poor nations aspire, and with which rich nations exist. Only a very few people are able to form anti-modern communes, intentional communities of dissatisfied customers who have rejected the depersonalization and crowded isolation of decaying cities. Kenneth Rexroth, who has made a sensitive survey of communalism over the centuries, has no illusions about the viability of such social structures. Most of these communities fail, although a few have thrived. It is very difficult to control sufficient sources of wealth (land, machinery, labor, diverse and complementary skills) without being deeply involved with the bureaucracy and technology of the dominant modern order, and without money to begin with. It is taxing to be alert and alive and unselfishly dedicated to a real concrete present task each day, when others directly depend on your industry. It is far easier to drop out of personal responsibility, which always translates as community responsibility, by joining some form of bureaucracy. When faced with immediate problems with other people, the hero of *The Red and the Black* ran away to either the army or the seminary, secure bureaucracies which would remove the burden of freedom and ease his passage for a while.

According to Rexroth, the few communes that succeed do so because they have heroic charismatic leaders, realistic choice of goals and use of resources, some transcendent belief that sustains their dedication in times of trial and temptation, and, finally, a source of recreation and joy and renewal within the community itself. Specialization of tasks beyond a certain point destroys a commune, Rexroth has found, because the link between the work and the life of the community becomes too abstract. Screening of potential members is also vital, because crackpots and malingerers just cannot be tolerated (although the sick and aged certainly can be).

Demodernization, where it is possible at all, requires a powerful will to achieve a free life of intense personal commitment and deep and enduring relationships. Depersonalization, for all the woe and raging loneliness it is accused of causing, seems to be preferred to demodernization. Since the Bible was begun, people have been leaving land and heading for cities.

As we have seen, the modernizing media have rushed in with paradoxical substitutes for community and companionship. In each instance the substitute is a professionally crafted general formula for everything from gossip to weather reports. Each of the professional "hosts" has the necessary geniality of the social director, remotely friendly and very much in charge. Glossy and graphic magazines, from *Viva* to *Vogue,* promote the production of conforming clones in appearance, consumer habits, and hobbies, just as the newsmagazines encourage formula assent to neatly wrapped issues. Relating so much of experience to a mass-produced product or process, Mediaworld only accelerates the depersonalizing mechanisms of modernism.

The professionalism, the legitimated procedures performed by certified celebrities, which the media have brought to the everyday functions once characteristic of communities, from conversation to sporting competition, have only reinforced the lonely-crowd conviction that real life, wherever it is, is elsewhere. Whatever is happening nearby and "uncovered" cannot ever be as real as what has been prepared by professional image-and-word merchants.

Lately this process has become so exaggerated that the media operatives assigned to cover, and thus make real, major events of a substantive nature actually outnumber the participants. Delegates to both major political conventions of 1976 and athletes at the 1976 Olympic Games were easily outnumbered by the reporters, novelists, poets, and film makers present. As a consequence, the event itself becomes transformed into a pseudo-event, since its shape and purpose are distorted to conform to media needs.

Modern international terrorists, whose existence is made possible by media technology and more likely by media policy on what is newsworthy, follow the dictates of media necessities. At times the deadlines set for the execution of hostages have been coordinated with optimal satellite transmission schedules to ensure more facile and more effective coverage. Mediaworld thus exacts an element of passivity from among the most active, even most desperate, individuals.

Such passivity makes it less and less likely that ordinary people can opt for a truly communal existence. The solution of problems through products as a constant theme, the substitution of show-business stars for charismatic leaders, the expectation of joy and renewal and recreation only coming from More of the Same, professionally provided from Elsewhere—all these marks of Mediaworld directly militate against the necessary conditions Rexroth has found true communalism requires. Spiritual emptiness seems at least in part a systematic necessity of Mediaworld.

fifteen
The Passing of the Flesh

Excess necessitates change. The bureaucracy of entertainment and the technology of opinion, the software we have chosen for our hardware, have exceeded mightily. In this they follow general historical patterns. Feudalism, mandarin rule, theocratic city-states, almost all forms of organization bear the seeds of their own destruction. Barry Commoner and Michael Harrington, among many others, have elegantly pointed out how the structures of modern technology and state-sponsored capitalism have reached critical stages of self-determined excess. Modernism is thus at an end and, with it, Mediaworld, the principal manifestation of the modernizing mentality (the instrument, if you will, of instrumentalism). In the state-sponsored capitalist system of America, this instrumentalism is chiefly incarnated in the marketing system.

Marketing and capitalism, like feudalism before them, brought many blessings to mankind. This book, however, has concentrated on the negative aspects of Mediaworld, as the showcase of symptoms for the terminal stages of modernism. For the Hebrews, the Flesh is a symbol of all the corrupting and corrupt elements of the human condition—a corruption that seems enduring. The Flesh, not to be confused with the human body, is always counterbalanced by the Spirit, the permanent quality of human life that strives to overcome the Flesh, to achieve justice, to create beauty, to find inner harmony. The organizing rubric for disparate aspects of modern communications institutions and their social settings that I have termed Mediaworld is the current principal form of the Flesh. It is passing. Like stages of life, periods of history begin to be understood as we are leaving them.

Whenever any prolonged negative criticism is made of the current situation, it has long been fashionable to respond with an even more stinging jeremiad against the evils of the times. After a slight pause, the source of the diatribe is triumphantly revealed as some disgruntled ancient from Greece or, more parochially, some concerned Colonial from the time of the American Revolution. Somehow our survival is seen as refutation of the critique, whose antiquity is presumed to be self-invalidating. To me it seems rather that the criticism of any time is as much a sign of the endurance of the Spirit as the conditions that provoke criticism are a testimony to the persistence of the Flesh. Survival is due to the balance.

Whatever form the next period of history takes—the Knowledge Society, the Age of Scarcity, Humane Socialism, the Technetronic Society—will place the Spirit and the Flesh in a different kind of dynamic tension. In any event, Mediaworld has considerable strength and power left and many years to run in terms of a human lifetime.

Residual faith in the redeeming potential of technology is still strong enough for many political and cultural radicals to see new kinds of media hardware, mostly miniaturized forms of videotape production and distribution, as liberating instruments capable of creating some sort of new media commune from the debris of the transitional forum. It is true that the new media require considerably less professional skill for operation. In this they follow a law of media technology development since printing: Lower skill demands on the user lead to more messages of diminishing significance or utility. It is unlikely that liberation will come from More of the Same with less professional skill.

Royal crowns and papal ceremony testify to the long heritage that links leadership with theatrical performance. Mediaworld modernized the link as a marriage between management and show business. Other forces, some of which we have sketched in these pages, have made the marriage obsessive and dangerous today. Insofar as records are available, it seems that Presidential press secretaries have become the most time-consuming, and perhaps the most heeded, consultants of the American head of state. As the forum that permits communication among contending groups, as well as between leaders and led, Mediaworld has elevated to an art form what has been called the "mystification of oppression." If mass addiction is lamentable, then leadership enchantment with manipulation through the media is truly frightening, whether it succeeds or not. The real world requires crisis-facing decisions that Mediaworld evades.

The evidence of the hard sciences about the health of earth's life-support systems is not encouraging. The political history of the modern nation-state and the current events managed by the emerging nations and the developed nations are no more encouraging. Nonetheless, we can derive some parochial hope from the new forms of regionalism and return to ethnic heritage that seem to mark a measured rejection of the excesses of modernism. Minor media and local community journalism are attracting young people of high skill and intelligence, who no longer see the major corporation or professional guilds as the inevitable framework for personal growth and social contributions. For future generations the very idea of the superstar may prove as bizarre as the tower-exile of Stylites, equally inhuman and remote. It is far too early to tell, but 1994 may be more humane than 1974 was or 1984 could be.

If it proves so, it will only be because we were able to outgrow Mediaworld.